NIHILISTIC TIMES

THE TANNER LECTURES ON HUMAN VALUES

NIHILISTIC TIMES

THINKING WITH MAX WEBER

WENDY BROWN

THE BELKNAP PRESS OF HARVARD UNIVERSITY PRESS

CAMBRIDGE, MASSACHUSETTS · LONDON, ENGLAND   2023

Library of Congress Cataloging-in-Publication Data

Names: Brown, Wendy, 1955– author.
Title: Nihilistic times : thinking with Max Weber / Wendy Brown.
Description: Cambridge, Massachusetts : The Belknap Press of Harvard
    University Press, 2023. | Includes bibliographical references and index.
Identifiers: LCCN 2022031722 | ISBN 9780674279384 (cloth)
Subjects: LCSH: Weber, Max, 1864–1920. | Citizenship—United States. |
    Nihilism (Philosophy)—Political aspects. | Identity politics—United States. |
    Ethics—United States.
Classification: LCC JF801 .B77 2023 | DDC 323.60973—dc23/eng/20220812
LC record available at https://lccn.loc.gov/2022031722

CONTENTS

NIHILISTIC TIMES

INTRODUCTION

This book is based on substantially revised and expanded versions of the Tanner Lectures on Human Values that I presented at Yale University in November 2019. The Tanner Lectures have no precise mandate, only a governing intellectual frame. Their benefactor and founder, Obert Clark Tanner, a British Mormon philosopher, lawyer, theologian, industrialist, and philanthropist, seemed to mirror his own unspecialized spirit in the loose rubric he offered for them in 1978: "I hope these lectures will contribute to the intellectual and moral life of mankind. I see them simply as a search for a better understanding of human behavior and human values."

Eventually, the rubric of the lectures was more narrowly circumscribed to "advance and reflect upon the scholarly and scientific learning relating to human values."[1] The circumscription sustains the ambiguous nomenclature of "values"—a nomenclature designating what we esteem or care for detached from the question of how or why, and a nomenclature so confessional of its status as an achievement or choice that the adjectival "human" is redundant except to underscore that values signify and perhaps secure an important dimension of humanness. However, the narrowing performs a different feat, which is to establish scholarship and science as distinct from, yet "relating" to, values. Is knowledge, then, imagined

1

as detached from values until specifically brought to bear on them, to scrutinize, philosophize, historicize, or otherwise understand them? Are values entailed by knowledge, embedded in knowledge, or merely informed or guided by knowledge? Is there also a conceit that to know the world—as scholars or scientists—is to know what to esteem within it?

The revised rubric of the Tanner Lectures, it would seem, still glides on Enlightenment assumptions about a distinction between truth and value, and about truth's capacity to inform value. It carries whiffs of the hope invested in this distinction and capacity, and especially in the idea that "learning" bears on the principles according to which life—individual and collective—ought to be lived. Yet it also throws us directly into the flood tide of modernity's other effects, where science first wrecked the foundations of value in God and tradition; then choked the redemptive value of value by elevating its economic meaning over others; then collapsed Enlightenment conceits about the link between knowledge and emancipation, knowledge and progress, knowledge and collective well-being, knowledge and choosing what to value or protecting what we value; and finally fell into crisis itself. What was science anyway if not a radically human production of one kind of truth *valued* above all others yet incapable of telling us what to value or how to craft the world accordingly?

All of this preceded our disorienting contemporary condition, in which philosophical, social, economic, ecological, and political coordinates for value and values are profoundly unsettled, both in knowledge practices and the world. There is today the rise of ferociously anti-democratic forces in settled as well as relatively newer liberal democracies, forces that openly affirm autocracy, theocracy, violent exclusions, or racial, ethnic, and gender supremacies. These emerge not only from far-right formations and parties but from assaults and corruptions of electoral systems from within and without, above and below—ranging from capture of politicians by dark money and capture of electorates by increasingly quotidian disinformation campaigns, to warping elections with voter suppression, gerrymandering, corporate funding, and foreign influence. There are the digital technologies continuously revolutionizing work, knowledge, governing, social relations, psyche, soma, and subjectivity, and bearing, along with enhancements of human capacities, novel ways of estranging, surveilling, and manipulating them. There is the political-economic transformation that unleashed finance as a force more powerful and less bound to human and planetary thriving than even capitalist commodity production. There is the chaos of the interregnum between the Westphalian global order and whatever might succeed it, a chaos marked by unprecedented boundary trespass *and* boundary policing of ideas, people, religions, capital, labor, technologies, violence, pollutants, and goods. And, there is the existential emergency posed by climate change, plummeting biodiversity, and the debris of a manic century of production piling up, unmetabolizable, in floating ocean islands and earthly fields of waste. This last includes more than a billion humans themselves cast off as waste: One in eight people now live in makeshift shanty towns, refugee or homeless camps within or abutting cities across the globe, with minimal access to civilizational basics—sanitation, nutrition, education, health care, and protection from the elements.

How to plot "values" within this disorienting present? On the one hand, we cannot orient ourselves exclusively by the compass points offered by established political-intellectual traditions. It is not only that the categories, concepts, and methods of these traditions are often inapt to the technologies, forms of capital, and climate emergency of our present, that they imagine the earth and human activity in an outmoded fashion. They are also saturated with the very assumptions and conceits generating many of our predicaments today. These range from a reckless anthropocentrism and racist, sexist humanisms, to rationalist or objectivist conceits of knowing and accounts of labor that exclude care work or accounts of "nature" that render it as passive material. They include deep ontological and epistemological oppositions—between nature and culture, fact and value, human and animal, animate and inanimate, civilized and barbaric—and more prosaic ones—between speech and action, or public and private.[2] They include formulations of time and space that disavow their often violent exclusionary, predatory, or colonial predicates. No discipline of knowledge, in its methods, contents, boundaries, or Weltanschauung, is immune to this upbraiding.

At the same time, *de novo* theorizing is its own fool's errand in trying to understand contemporary predicaments and possibilities within it, and this for at least two reasons. First, intelligent reckonings with our singular present must be historically minded. Even as we chart certain novel powers, technologies, subjectivities, and political formations today, we must also reckon with the long historical forces that frame and intersect them—among them nihilism, capitalism, patriarchy, white supremacy—

INTRODUCTION

themselves transforming as they engage multiple effects of globalization and climate change. Second, this complicated reckoning, at once deeply historical and appreciative of the distinctiveness of the present, is often abetted by studies of earlier theorists. This abetting occurs not by applying past thinkers' analytics of power, diagnoses of conditions, historiographies, or strategies for change to our predicaments but by thinking with and against them about these predicaments. There is something else. Many enduring social and political theorists are such not only because they invented profound and illuminating new frameworks, but because they were actively struggling for a cartography of their own disorienting times. We are not the first in history to wrestle with the problem that humans have never been here before: only the "here" is singular.

This is what brings me to think with Max Weber in these pages, and in particular with his well-known lectures on knowledge and politics, conventionally rendered in English as "Science as a Vocation" and "Politics as a Vocation." In these lectures, delivered at the request of University of Munich students in 1917 and 1919, Weber draws the contours, predicaments, and potentials of both domains in an era he regarded as rapidly draining of meaning and integrity, and threatened by descent into "a polar night of icy darkness and harshness."[3] His searing indictments of the university in his time—its patronage system of hiring and promotion, its corrosively politicized scholarship and classrooms, its anti-Semitic and other exclusion of promising young scholars, its invasion by capitalist values, its low standards for teaching, and its hyper-specialization that withdrew scholarly work from worldliness—echo some features of our own. Weber's portrait of the conditions for aspiring politicians of integrity and purpose also was bleak and also has contemporary resonance: He depicted a political sphere populated with demagogues and bureaucrats but few genuine leaders, and dominated by party machines and manipulated masses. He cast democracy as unviable beyond a plebiscitary form and function. And he formulated political life in modernity as necessarily filled with permanently warring and undecidable values, themselves saturated with the distinctly political currencies of force and fraud.

These notes of relevance notwithstanding, thinking with Weber now will also seem counterintuitive, if not perverse, to many. Weber is often held responsible for setting twentieth-century social science knowledge on a dangerous and hubristic course of faux objectivity and ethical neutrality, along with the intense knowledge specialization and insulated disciplinary methods deterring the very knowledge practices required to understand and criticize rather than mirror and ratify the status quo. He is conventionally associated with founding the hard fact-value distinction underlying a century of positivism, not only identifying the one with truth (however provisional, given unending scientific progress) and the other with subjective judgment, but insisting that science could and must be value free. He is famous for charting varieties of action and authority in a conservative mode, drawing and valorizing ideal types, founding a problematic sociology of religion, challenging Marxism with an account of capitalism's origins in Protestantism, and theorizing the rationalization and disenchantment of the world wrought by secular modernity in a manner that is now challenged by new materialists, philosophers of science, and theorists of the secular alike. Notorious for straightjacketing the social sciences with his anti-normative mandates, refusing the depths of the hermeneutics he avowed, and defining politics narrowly, he is rarely adopted as a friend of critical theory today even as the early Frankfurt School and Foucault both drew on his thought. Politically, Weber is ordinarily regarded as sanguine about capitalism, state power, and competition among sovereign nation states. He is identified with intense German nationalism, anxious masculinism, and early attraction to that peculiar strain of neoliberalism that would later come to imprint the European unification project with undemocratic principles and techniques.[4] He glorifies *Machtpolitik* and praises states and politicians who embrace it. He is considered not merely a realist but ardent anti-idealist, in both political and intellectual life.

Given these attributions, Weber may appear complicit with if not an architect of some of the most sinister forces contouring our present. The above synopsis, however, is a reductionist account of Weber's complex formulations of knowledge, history, politics, capitalism, and power. It ignores much of the ambivalence, complexity, subtlety, originality, and internal intellectual conflict that makes Weber invaluable to think *with*. These features are especially on display in the Vocation Lectures he delivered near the end of his life, the focus of my reflections here.

Weber was a dark thinker. This was not only a matter of his dominion, temperament, or times, though certainly each was treacherous. As important was his unrivaled appreciation of certain logics of modernity: its signature rationalities and forms of power; its generation of "human machineries" with unprecedented capacities for domination; its simultaneous proliferation and depreciation of value and values (its reduction of morality to matters of taste); the inadequacy of democracy to resist or transform these developments, and the great challenge of cultivating responsible teaching and political leadership amid them. In a world he viewed as choked by powers destructive of human spirit and freedom as well as forthrightly dangerous, he sought to craft practices by which both scholars and political actors might hold back the dark with their work, and perhaps model purpose, or tender hope, in the fading light for each. This is one reason for turning to him now. We need sober thinkers who refuse to submit to the lures of fatalism or apocalypticism, pipe dreams of total revolution or redemption by the progress of reason, yet aim to be more than Bartlebys or foot soldiers amid current orders of knowledge and politics.

A second reason for turning to Weber pertains to his confrontation, early in the interwar period, with crises of political and academic life bearing certain parallels to our own, including a crisis of liberalism. Intellectually, Weber took Marx and Nietzsche to be major intellectual influences of his time, and though he regarded each as profound, he also saw them as dangerously wrongheaded and sought to repel anti-liberal critiques from the Left and the Right that each inspired.[5] Politically, Weber took Germany in particular and Europe in general to be endangered by radical mass movements; by vain demagogues; by irresponsible nationalists and socialists; and by bureaucratic-legal statism—technocracies fantasized by academics and embraced by some politicians.[6] Weber's response to this condition was not to rehabilitate the liberal statesman or representative.[7] Rather, it was to cultivate an ideal of leaders as *rulers,* and in turn to task rulers with the pursuit of a political vision, responsibly pursued. He invested hope in those who would honor electoral democracy, the rule of law, and liberal limits on government while artfully using their power and persuasion to build political futures that could slip the constraints of bureaucratic administration, let alone socialist statism, and push beyond the stalemates of liberal democratic compromise and logrolling.[8] If, today, we face bowdlerized versions of this on the right (Bolsonaro, Trump, Orbán, Erdoğan, Modi), we may still want to ask about this possibility on the left.[9] Whether aspiring to rescue or throw in the towel on liberal democracy, left-political mobilizations have become increasingly engaged by the question of leadership for large-scale transformations that exceed parliamentary tinkering but are short of revolution. This is true of left populism, green democratic socialism, abolitionist and Indigenous politics. This makes Weber's unblinking confrontation with the crisis of liberalism and democracy in his time, especially in "Politics as a Vocation," potentially illuminating for one we face a century later.[10]

A third reason for thinking with Weber now, and the main one animating these essays, pertains to his deep confrontation with the intellectual and political predicaments of our nihilistic epoch. The pervasive nihilism that disinhibits aggression and devalues values (compounding neoliberal depredations of democracy, social responsibility, and concern with future generations) was the problem with which I concluded *In the Ruins of Neoliberalism* without plotting a way through it.[11] If Weber is better known for his formalizations of methods and ideal types, folding hermeneutics into objective studies of social action, and his unique reformulation of materialist history to feature the centrality of values, this list occludes his effort to combat nihilistic effects in both knowledge and politics. This feature of his thought is overtly signaled by his frequent allusions to Tolstoy's conclusion that in modernity, death and hence life are meaningless, and to Dostoyevsky's portrait of the ethical irrationality of the world. It appears in his concerns with the effects of disenchantment, rationalization, boundary breakdowns, and the ubiquity of vanity or narcissism in intellectual, political, and cultural life. Hardly nihilism's most complex theorist—Nietzsche, Heidegger, Adorno, Rorty, Rosen, and Pippin offer richer philosophical accounts—Weber may be among its most political. He formulates nihilism as contributing to the condition of contemporary politics and at the same time identifies politics as a vital platform for nihilism's overcoming: politics is the quintessential domain for articulating and pursuing what he calls "ultimate values" or worldviews, not merely power or interest. His adamant fact-value distinction in social science research and classrooms is also set against nihilism's door, where truth and deliberation, not only morality and ethics, are at risk of being abandoned.

There are many ways to account for the contemporary rise of antidemocratic popular forces and the opportunistic masters of power politics drawing succor from them in the West today. Only one of these would feature the political expression of nihilism, a plant Nietzsche predicted would take two hundred years to bloom from the grave of deities and ideals toppled by science and the Enlightenment.[12] Nihilism is manifest today as ubiquitous moral chaos or disingenuousness but also as assertions of power and desire shorn of concern for accountability to truth, justice, consequences, or futurity, not only ethics. Nihilism is revealed in the careless, even festive, breaking of a social compact with others and with succeeding generations that is manifest in quotidian speech and conduct today, especially but not only on the right. It appears in witting indifference to a fragile planet and fragile democracies. It manifests, too, as normalized deceit and criminality in both high and low places, and as mass withdrawal into the trivial, immediate, and personal.[13] It is evident in the strategic drape of "traditional morality" over political aims to resecure historical supremacies of race, gender, and ownership or aims to capture electorates attracted to these supremacies. It is inscribed in the ubiquitous practices of "reputation repair" and the shifting-with-the-winds opportunism of even the most self-serious public figures. It is expressed in unprecedented popular indifference to consistency, accountability, and even veracity in religious and political leaders. It appears in the shrill epistemological standoff between Right and Left: the ferocious defense of religion and tradition on the one side, reason and progress on the other, with neither giving quarter *or* avowing the quicksand in which their flags are planted and on which their battle is played out. Far from exhaustive, this list is limited to nihilism's public life.

The question for those who want to draw the planet, democracy, and care for justice back from the brink: What prospects are there for a politics that could overcome, dispel, or work through nihilism, or at the very least, repel or end-run its most severe effects?[14] And how might knowledge— generating it, curating it, and transmitting it—be protected from nihilistic forces, or better, employed for their overcoming? These are among the questions Weber confronted directly in the Vocation Lectures.

By nihilism, I am not suggesting, nor was Weber, that all value has disappeared from the world, or that life is widely held to be without any purpose or meaning. Understood as a condition rather than a contingent attitude, nihilism both emerges from modernity and generates distinct predicaments for meaning within it. On the one hand, it is difficult to find criteria, let alone foundations, for meaning and value without appealing to discredited sources for those foundations—religion, tradition, or logic—a discrediting that makes such appeals inevitably reactionary and shrill.[15] On the other hand, faith in progress is revealed as a secularized version of the Christian millennium and as empirically confounded by modernity's failure to deliver generalized peace, prosperity, happiness, or freedom. When appeals to origins and telos thus falter, programs for change themselves lose their compass, as if, in Nietzsche's words, "we unchained the earth from its sun."[16] Now we are spinning without tether or illumination, without certain knowledge about what to affirm and negate, without temporality or directionality for a motion of history. Under these conditions, purpose and judgment alike are stripped naked, unbearably so.

There is more. For Weber, scholarly knowledge (*Wissenschaft,* often translated as science but comprising all systematic and transmissible academic knowledge, including in the humanities) undercuts the basis of religion but not its continued existence. Rather, in a rational and rationalized world, Weber declares matter-of-factly, to be religious requires a necessary "sacrifice of the intellect," by which he means that religion must reject science on the most fundamental question of how we know what we know.[17] Rebuffing the Nietzschean suggestion that science, too, rests on a sandy bottom and can attract devotion in weak religious fashion, Weber goes a different way: as science topples religion from the throne of Truth, it does not and cannot replace religion's meaning-making power. This limitation of science changes the nature, reach, and implications of Truth; it is what splits fact from value and makes the latter undecidable at a scholarly level. Science can unveil the mysteries of the world—the process Weber calls disenchantment—but cannot generate or rank values.[18] Science can never create value, Nietzsche writes, making it "the best ally the ascetic ideal has at present" with its "object of dissuading man from his former respect for himself."[19] Weber quotes Tolstoy: "Science is meaningless because it has no answer to the only questions that matter to us: 'What should we do? How shall we live?'"[20] Utilitarian calculation may reveal what ends are lost as others are pursued but cannot decide the question of what matters or why. It cannot answer Tolstoy's questions. When it pretends that it can, as happens with neoliberal norms of value, governing, and conduct, a new threshold of nihilism is reached, one Weber anticipated without knowing what its precise form might be.[21]

As science unmoors meaning from its religious and moral foundations, for Weber, values are also eroded from another source in his time, namely the overtaking of what he calls "value rationality" with "instrumental rationality" in every quarter of life. This overtaking is enabled by the freedom from ethical constraint of instrumental reason, and it gains ground by virtue of this form's sheer power over modes of thought and action where means and ends remain bound together. Weber's theory of the raw power released by separating means from ends undergirds his understanding of the machinery of capitalism (where workers are separated from the ends of production) and bureaucracy (where bureaucrats are separated from the overall function of an organization). It also structures his formulation of rationalization and secularization as systemic forces rather than the consequence of subjective intention or aim. But if sundering means from ends generates unprecedented quantities of power through efficiencies, it also diminishes and ultimately devours ends. Everything becomes an instrument, and power begets only more power, wealth only more wealth, calculation only more calculation. Instrumental reason itself is embodied in giant "human machineries" becoming our "iron cages" and converting what originated as a means for meeting needs into an order of domination.[22] In this way too, more than merely independent of value, instrumental reason bears an innate tendency to destroy value, overtaking ends it was designed to serve or converting ends themselves into means, ultimately eviscerating values everywhere with instrumental rationality.[23] Financialization and digitalization are the latest instances of what started as instruments morphing into apparatuses of domination beyond human control, now also so powerful that they could crash the world into catastrophe overnight.

In sum, for Weber, in modernity, on the one hand, all meaning is revealed as made, not discovered, and values are undecidable. On the other hand, established meanings are relentlessly unmade by forces of disen-chantment and rationalization, respectively the usurpation of myth and mystery by science and the cannibalization of ends by means in an instru-mentally rational world. This much is familiar. The problem of nihilism for Weber, however, exceeds the value-depleting powers of disenchant-ment and rationalization. Rather, *it rests in the consequential intervals opened up between knowledge, politics, and religion in modernity,* and es-pecially the partitions—sometimes even oppositions—developed between science and religion, politics and religion, and knowledge and politics. In modernity, knowledge must feature the value-neutrality generative of objectivity; politics features value struggle combined with steely-eyed appreciation that this struggle comprises human rather than divine powers and purposes; and religion rebuffs both sets of assumptions to affirm knowledge and values originating in and delivered by otherworldly powers.

Notwithstanding its historical recency, this distinctly modern separa-tion of spheres and of the principles legitimating each is what Weber seeks to fortify and police. This can be seen at once in the way that Weber shapes the vocations for science and politics in his two lectures. On the one hand, he distances these vocations from one another and from a vocation for religion. On the other, he infuses each with a secularized religious spirit, one that both animates and ethically constrains the practitioner. Drawing the notion of *Beruf* (calling or vocation) from its embeddedness in the Protestant imperative to serve God through earthly work, he iterates the post-secular calling for each sphere as bound not to God but to the devotion, convictions, and sacrifices constituting remainders of religious practice and feeling after the divinity is gone. Only the claim of such a spiritual-ethical force, lingering after we have lost the Supreme Being, can prevent the descent of political and knowledge practices into raw self-gratification or raw will to power.

Beruf, as Weber crafts it in a post-nihilist dispositional mode, entails near superhuman commitments to selflessness, maturity, restraint, and responsibility combined with passionate dedication to a cause outside the self. *Beruf* casts the subject neither as mere vessel for a vocation nor as served and gratified by it, but rather as *realized* through it. This said, the separation of religion from *Wissenschaft* and politics in modernity strips religion itself of accountability to truth *or* power.[24] Thus, when the religious-minded do not stay in their quarter but attempt to exercise epistemological or practical power in the political or knowledge domain, the effect is a special kind of corruption, one Weber anoints as nihilistic. To put the matter the other way around, paradoxically, the only responsible actor in a nihilistic age, and the only one able to carry us beyond the age, is one who fully confronts the predicaments of meaning making today and rises to the challenge of creating meaning in a world absent its givenness.[25] If modernity is structured by unbridgeable chasms between knowledge and purpose, and between knowledge and belief, only those who can face these chasms, and craft their passions and endeavors in both an ethical and courageous relationship to them, are capable of being responsible scholars or political actors. Only those who have confronted the lack of moral absolutes in public life and the inappropriateness of turning to science or religion for those absolutes will bring integrity and ethical accountability to any of the three spheres that have parted from each other—religion, scholarship, politics.

Furthermore, for Weber, the absence of foundations for values simultaneously reveals them as inherently imbricated with power, contestable *and* available to critical analysis even if they do not spring from reason or refer to it for legitimacy. These same features are what make values essentially political—both contingent and power-laden—and also make politics *the* domain for struggling over them and for them. (If Nietzsche tasks philosophy with generating post-nihilist value, Weber refuses this tasking precisely in order to protect knowledge from politics. For him, the academy is a place to coolly analyze the presumptions and implications of warring value systems, not the place to spawn or promulgate them.) More than only infected by nihilism in modernity, which it is, politics for Weber is the distinctive venue for countering nihilism's dangerous potential inversion into indifference or worse—fatalism, cynicism, frivolity, narcissism, or non-accountable deployments of power and violence. In a secular, rationalized, and nihilistic age, when religious and cultural authority have disintegrated, politics acquires unprecedented importance for the articulation, justification, contestation, and pursuit of values. Put another way, when nihilism is full-blown, ultimate values are at once politicized in a trivial way and at the same time enlarged as the ultimate stakes of political struggle. On the one hand, ubiquitous politicization (today, for example, of consumption, diet, pastimes, pleasures, style, family form, parenting practices, lifestyle, even body type) is itself a symptom of nihilism. On the other hand, formal political life is a theater of nihilism: the political sphere is where nihilism is played out in raw form *and also* a site for overcoming or pushing back against nihilism through pursuit of worldly causes. In our time, both potentials are there, and routinely collide.

The paradox of the political sphere as ravaged by nihilism *and* as a venue for overcoming nihilism arises because, for Weber, the domain of the political is quintessentially partisan. It is by nature a sphere of contestation (over meanings and not only aims) rather than of objectivity, though it is not therefore purely subjective or reducible to interest.[26] The relentlessly partisan nature of political life binds politics to struggles over values, but the inherently non-foundational character of values in modernity binds value to politics. Thus, Sheldon Wolin comments, for Weber, "values came to be the symbolic equivalent of politics," which is why he sequestered them from knowledge production and teaching.[27] But the reverse is also true: values are irreducible in politics and cannot be extinguished without extinguishing political life as such. Weber saw this threat of extinction in the possibility that politics might be overwhelmed by bureaucracy or reduced to administration, technocracy, raw interest, or power play. Moreover, as values diversify consequent to the breakdown of moral authority in modernity, politics becomes ever more important in mediating or brokering value conflicts.[28] Thus, while Weber understood politics in his time to be saturated with nihilistic effects, he also saw its unique potential as a domain for articulating, mobilizing, and struggling over the question of how we should live together after answers rooted in tradition or moral-religious foundations have been undone by the related yet distinct forces of disenchantment and rationalization. At the same time, since the currency of politics is power, its ultimate instrument is violence, and its essence is partisanship, there can be no political neutrality, objectivity, or peace *ever*. The value struggles unfolding in its domain are eternal—cold comfort for those still invested in narratives of progress, not to mention harmony or epistemic universality.

This is the capsule version of my interpretation of Weber, and of why I think Weber's wrestle with nihilism in politics and knowledge is useful to our predicaments in both realms today, even as we may—and I will— disagree with the prescriptions and prohibitions Weber offered in response to the condition he charted so perspicaciously. Even as we may challenge his stipulations of the very nature of knowledge (objective) and politics (state centered). And even as we may want to mobilize his insights for phenomena he abjured, such as left-political mobilizations or deep democratization.[29]

In the ensuing chapters, I consider each lecture in turn: first politics, then science / knowledge. This reverses the order in which Weber composed and delivered his lectures—Science in November 1917, then Politics in January 1919—but reflecting on them in this order surfaces the broader post-nihilist project that Weber tacitly, perhaps even unconsciously, builds across these two realms. One additional note: the reader will not find a Weber scholar behind these reflections. I am indebted to the scholarship, of course, but my purpose is not to contribute to it. Rather, my aim is to think with Weber for our times, for our disturbed and disturbing world.

ONE | POLITICS

[W]hat is possible could never have been achieved unless people
had tried again and again to achieve the impossible in this world . . .
even those who are neither a leader nor a hero must arm themselves with that staunchness of heart that refuses to be daunted by
the collapse of all their hopes.

—MAX WEBER

Politics means a slow, powerful drilling through hard boards.

—MAX WEBER

In contemporary popular parlance,
nihilism is an attitude in which everything, human life above all, is without
essential meaning or value. An individual *Weltanschauung* variously attributed to punk, terrorism, adolescent ennui, postmodernism, and some
forms of depression, it is associated affectively with hopelessness about
the future, cynicism, pessimism, relativism, or despair. It is also often
identified with irresponsibility, power without right, guiltless criminality,
and indifference to suffering. Certainly nihilism carries all of these possibilities. However, nihilism as a condition—precipitated by various forces
of European modernity and especially the Enlightenment challenge to
divine authority, and recently intensified by neoliberal economization of
all value and by technologies of artificial intelligence—is something else.

For Weber and Nietzsche, nihilism is Western modernity's inevitable excrescence, generated when religious truth and the values it secures are displaced by reason and science. If premodern authority were not mono-theistic, if the Supreme Being were not omniscient and omnipotent, and if reason were not the rival and then replacement for God, meaning would not have been cast into crisis with the Enlightenment. Religious and tradi-tional authority would not have been unseated by science, and reason would not have been sought to replace religious wellsprings of meaning. But not only is this a difficult "if" to imagine, it is also irrelevant to European modernity, which Nietzsche and Weber understand to have emerged from a secular transformation of the religious foundations of the West. These founda-tions, assaulted by unparalleled powers of science, calculative and instru-mental reason, capital, state power, and more, were not simply vanquished by this assault but broken into ruins that continue to order the landscape. Nihilism thus takes root, and then flight, from the specific predicament for meaning arising from the prolonged modern crisis of monotheism in the West.[1] However, its capacities for contagion and for sedimentation in insti-tutions and practices in excess of this original drive contribute to spreading nihilism across the contemporary social and political landscape.

NIETZSCHE

Weber's account of nihilism draws from Nietzsche's but charts the effects differently and stages a different struggle against it. For Nietzsche, nihilism is a cultural-historical condition born of the toppling of God and accompanying recognition that neither secularized religion nor its cousins, science and reason, secure meaning for human existence or human endeavor. This recognition, *as long as it is still captured by the condition that produced it,* generates a conviction that life itself is meaningless and without value, which Nietzsche resists by tasking us with constructing and legislating meaning apart from moral systems rooted in otherworldly foundations. Nihilism is the state we fall into after these otherworldly foundations are shattered, but before the secular task of creating or "legislating" value is embraced. Nietzsche therefore identifies nihilism as "a pathological transitional stage"—the pathology pertains to "the tremendous generalization, the inference that there is no meaning at all" from this particular crisis of meaning.[2] "One interpretation has perished; but because it was regarded as *the* interpretation," Nietzsche writes, "there now seems to be no meaning at all in existence, everything seems to be *in vain.*"[3]

In this historical-cultural condition, accepting that we are "value-positing" creatures is equally difficult for religious believers and atheists. Nietzsche writes:

> The nihilistic question "for what?" is rooted in the old habit of supposing that the goal must be put up, given, demanded *from outside—* by some *superhuman authority*. Having unlearned faith in that, one still follows the old habit and seeks *another* authority that can *speak unconditionally* and *command* goals and tasks. The authority of *conscience* now steps up front (the more emancipated one is from theology, the more imperativistic morality becomes) to compensate for

> the loss of a *personal* authority. Or the authority of *reason*. Or the *social instinct* (the herd). Or *history* with an immanent spirit and a goal within, so one can entrust oneself to it. . . . Finally, *happiness*—and with a touch of Tartuffe, *the happiness of the greatest number.*[4]

We can spy other substitutes for the old authority today—for example, belief in the transcendent truth of markets, of social justice, of nature, of heteropatriarchy, of humanism or anti-humanism. For now, however, let us stay with Nietzsche's larger claim that while these substitutes aim to repel a nihilist conclusion, they actually express, even symptomatize, a world that has lost its mooring in the givenness of meaning. Here is one of Nietzsche's most compressed accounts of this phenomenon:

> The feeling of valuelessness was reached on understanding that neither the concept of 'purpose', nor the concept of 'unity', nor the concept of 'truth' may be used to interpret the character of existence. Nothing is aimed for and achieved with it; there is no overarching unity in the diversity of events; the character of existence is not 'true', is false. . . . One simply no longer has any reason to talk oneself into there being a *true* world. . . . In short: the categories 'purpose', 'unity', 'being', by means of which we put a value into the world, we now *extract* again—and now the world *looks valueless.*[5]

Again, the world that *appears* valueless is an effect of a particular history, a history featuring the collapse of a specific theology. This appearance is neither the truth of existence nor the truth about values but, rather, an outcome of this process. Thus Nietzsche continues:

> Assuming we have recognized how the world may no longer be *inter-preted* with these three categories [purpose, unity, being] and that upon this recognition the world begins to be without value for us: then we must ask *where* our belief in these three categories came from—let us see if it isn't possible to cancel our belief in *them*. Once we have *devaluated* these three categories, demonstrating that they can't be applied to the universe *ceases to be a reason to devaluate the universe*.[6]

Hence we note the importance of *revaluation* to conducting genealogies of our moral principles, and to perceiving how we might recover from the nihilism at the conclusion of such a genealogy. Revaluation requires challenging received understandings of the origin of values, the interests they serve, and the formations they incite, a challenge famously reprised in the preface to *Genealogy of Morals*.[7]

The difficulty of re-founding value in nihilistic times, however, exceeds the task of overcoming conceits about origin, unity, and telos. Rather, at the heart of this difficulty is what nihilism does to value. For Nietzsche, nihilism *devalues* values, including the value of truth itself, while keeping them around. "The goal is lacking; an answer to the question 'why?' What does nihilism mean? That the highest values are devaluated."[8] With their foundation eroded but their formulas and insignias lingering, values do not simply evaporate but become malleable, fungible, trivial, instrumentalizable, easily trafficked for purposes beyond themselves, and at the same time histrionic and hyperbolic.[9] Nietzsche calls this "decadence," and contemporary examples abound in commerce, politics, religion, and the ostentatious branding of everything and everyone with superficial iterations of cultural or social values. When values become capital enhancing, as they are today for individuals, corporations, non-profits, cities, and states alike, and when they are attached to objects ranging from investment choices to coffee choices to athletic heroes, their trivialization and instrumentalization reach a nadir even Nietzsche did not anticipate. Inscribed as hash tags, bumper stickers, yard signs, ephemeral group identities, or advertising bait, values lose their depth and endurance, their relationship to a *Weltanschauung*, their wholesale governing of conduct and conscience, their capacity to shape moral order. Beyond indexing cultural divides, brands identified with feminism, anti-racism, anti-colonialism, and non-normative gender on the one side, and with God, heteronormative families, and patriotism on the other, signal values made hollow and hucksterish by nihilism.

For Nietzsche, the devaluation of values also entails a radical reduction in the force of conscience. How does this go? The sublimation of instincts or desires (both primal and historically and culturally shaped—Nietzsche's finesse!) that authoritative values demand is lightened or even reversed, and anti-social eruptions are the result. Here, Nietzsche's thesis is close to Freud's, and again, examples abound: disinhibition, especially of aggression, is everywhere. The "conscience" at the heart of the liberal democratic social compact, however compromised throughout its history, is now overtly thrown off: both legislative and popular commitments to fairness, inclusion, the rule of law, and to future generations are casually jettisoned and sometimes overtly attacked. Other effects of a nihilistic condition according to Nietzsche include hyper-individualism and presentism. The social compact with others and with past and future broken, we fall into a world of one and a world of now. Again, this formation dovetails neatly with neoliberal encomiums of the past half century: indeed, nihilism both facilitates the neoliberal economization of everything and is intensified by this economization. Still, Hobbes's declaration that "the value of a man is his price" was penned in the seventeenth century, vindicating Nietzsche's insistence that nihilism was born with modernity, not with its waning.[10]

Truth, Nietzsche argues, is devalued along with every other value in a nihilistic age.[11] More than merely strategically overwhelmed by propaganda, fused with commerce, manipulated by opportunistic demagogues or Russian troll farms, and shattered by the drive for clickbait, truth—and its cousins, honesty, integrity, and accountability—cannot survive value's degrounding and diminution. In fact, this degrounding and diminution reveal truth *as* a value, one sometimes imbricated with facticity but hardly reducible to it.[12] So also does the antagonism between science and religion abet truth's slide; if religion does not have truth but is rooted in faith and need, then it also does not want, admire, or burnish truth. Yet its unclasping from truth makes religion perversely wanton, promiscuous, an inconstant governor of ways of life and available to a special kind of politicization, about which more shortly.[13]

The broad cultural and political devaluation of truth generates a range of possible affective-intellectual orientations, including cynicism, skepticism, pessimism, and even romanticism. The major divide for Nietzsche is between those who repudiate religion and those who cling to it. What he calls the "pale atheists" dwell in irony, skepticism, and above all, themselves. Certainly narcissism is a boom industry in a nihilistic age, as is cultivating and satisfying appetites. With all value diminished, only immediate gratifications and security remain compelling. Today these nihilistic effects—absorption with the self, and its desires and safety—comport closely with the governing rationality of both neoliberalism and securitarian authoritarianism, explaining the ease with which both have displaced democracy.[14] Ardent religionists, on the other hand, clutch their crosses and refuse intellection, making them easily available to fictions posing as truths and mobilization by demagogues. Both tendencies, narcissistic self-indulgence and religion without depth or consistency, express what Robert Pippin terms the *failure of desire* that is nihilism, its lost want of world, of the other, or even of its own life.[15] Again, Nietzsche: "the aim is lacking."

For Nietzsche, working through nihilism to differently orient oneself to the death of God involves culturing value at a deep and non-reactive level and seeking to "legislate" values in and for the world. This renewal of value does not arise from deliberation or calculative choice but, rather, shares the non-rational, non-strategic character of Eros. In Robert Pippin's formulation, "Something grips us, something we cannot help caring about; it would not be love if it were in the service of some instrumental strategy, and . . . far more than simply a felt desire. It involves a wholehearted passionate commitment to and identification with a desired end."[16] Overcoming nihilism does not mean deciding rationally what to value across a diverse order of objects and possibilities (which would in any case hoist the fiction of that "little changeling, the subject . . . the doer behind the deed, the neutral substratum before willing") but culturing value from a wellspring of passionate attachment, thus repairing the failure of desire and aim that is nihilism.[17] Of course this culturing can be shaped by education, influence, or experience, and in fact must counter the formation that is our found condition—it remains reactive if it is only what the psychoanalysts call "acting out." So not just any passionate attachment will do. Still, that passion is now placed at the root of value means its post-nihilist version is divorced not only from divine or any other absolute authority, but from culturally hegemonic reproduction *and* saturation at the site of what we commonly call tradition. Post-nihilist value is without foundations that would secure its truth and without a homogenous culture everywhere generating and reflecting it. Even if widely accepted and successfully legislated ("legislating new values" is how Nietzsche characterizes moving beyond nihilism), this novelty remains. Such inversion of the origin of value, from inculcation by world to overt legislation by power, is one reason Max Weber will locate post-nihilist regeneration of value at the site of charismatic leadership.[18] Not only God but tradition is finished as a stable source of authority in modernity, and rational-legal authority is no more capable than science of generating value. Only charismatic power, whose *anima* is dedication to a cause, and whose allure is its vision, but which may operate apart from religion, has the political potential to move, and to move its followers, through and beyond nihilism.

WEBER

Before pursuing this further, we need to pause over Weber's account of the historical condition of nihilism, one that draws on yet diverges from Nietzsche's and resists some of Nietzsche's solutions. Nietzsche's influence on Weber was strong, but Tolstoy's work, and perhaps even Tolstoy's personal crisis of nihilistic despair, was also important as Weber developed his own perspective on nihilistic effects in culture, politics, and knowledge. Above all, for Weber, the disintegrating foundation for authoritative values does not only weaken and trivialize values but proliferates and diversifies them.[19] The authority that would secure a single and common truth gone, we live now, Weber says, as the Ancients did when they "would bring a sacrifice at one time to Aphrodite and at another to Apollo . . . only now the gods have been deprived of the magical and mythical but inwardly true qualities that gave them such vivid immediacy."[20] Weber's invocation of the Greeks is laden: with ultimate values undecidable, we are returned to a certain pre-modern, pre-Christian condition, one that breaks the Enlightenment promise by dethroning rather than crowning truth in the domain of value.

Having lost its ground in truth, and supported neither by science nor capitalism, liberalism, along with the principles it subtends, becomes deeply and dangerously vulnerable.[21] (Both Nietzsche and Weber would groan at the "marketplace of ideas" often hailed as truth's determinant today, as if markets and truth were ever related, as if markets secure and refine rather than abuse and degrade truth, and as if targeting and trolling had not become permanent features of all marketplaces, including those of ideas.[22]) Nothing guarantees liberalism's survival, or that of democracy, when, as Weber puts it, "each individual has to decide for himself which . . . is the devil and which the God *for him*."[23] Moreover, as values proliferate, diversify, and cheapen, peoples and nations will be inevitably splintered and riven. Our nomenclatures for this condition—"culture wars" or political polarization—mistake effect for cause and therefore do not capture the historical condition Weber charts. For Weber, crumbled authority for moral or political judgment is primary in deracinating values; secularization and rationalization accelerate their corrosion or cheapening. From this perspective, the religious-secular, rural-urban, or reactionary-emancipatory divides so often posited by contemporary pundits are expressions, not drivers, of this condition.

Both broken or spurned norms generated by value deracination and social conflict generated by value proliferation are nihilistic effects. So also is a specific kind of hyper-politicization: *everything* becomes iconic of contesting political worldviews or is branded within this contest.[24] Today this hyper-politicization (hence trivialization) of values reaches to consumption practices, family forms, home decor, gun ownership, school curriculums, sports preferences and athletes, ecological practices, fashion, sexual practices, gender presentation, diet and exercise. Beyond indexing the cheapening of values, which it does, such hyper-politicization also imports the cardinal currencies of politics—force, fraud, and manipulation of appearances—into every domain. Everywhere a crude Machiavellianism prevails. The inverse is also in play: moral values and knowledge themselves become instrumentalized for power purposes, an instrumentalization that further degrades the integrity and worth of both. At the same time, law and religion shed even the pretense of non-political status. (Consider quotidian politicization of judicial appointments, interpretations, and decisions, on the one hand, and bids by organized religion to throw off legal constraints on political engagement, on the other.) Together these effects deepen skepticism about truth, moral stances, the integrity of faith, and the value of law as neutral arbiter and protector. That skepticism in turn intensifies the whorl of nihilistic forces.

Finally, there is what Mark Warren formulates as Weber's implicit thesis of "bureaucratic nihilism" or "bureaucracy as an institutionalized form of nihilism" in secular orders.[25] Since bureaucracies (and today technocracies) are built on the separation of means and ends, and exist to promote purely technical efficiency, they cannot embody "value rationality." They are formally indifferent to value, although of course this does not make them norm-free in practice. These features of bureaucracy acquire nihilistic force when bureaucracies come to dominate spheres like politics rather than merely serve political aims, when the machinery of state becomes the state, and swallows and subverts political leadership with bureaucratic enmeshment. Moreover, as this power undercuts that of leaders and institutions alike, "they make what are in fact irresponsible political decisions under the guise of technical expertise."[26] The inherent soullessness of bureaucracy increasingly displaces not only value-driven decision making and action, but values themselves.

Given Weber's attunement to the multiple sources of nihilism in contemporary political life, how and why for Weber could the political sphere be a domain for resisting or overcoming nihilism? How, as religious and moral authority wane, and politics itself is saturated with nihilistic effects, and those effects keep ramifying, could political life become a theater for renewing value and for rebuilding the human integrity required to sustain and live by substantive values? Weber's genius in "Politics as a Vocation" is to drive straight into the predicaments of nihilism, and to insist that political leadership take its bearings and develop its ethics from these predicaments, especially from the loss of moral foundations *and* the permanent imbrication of all political purposes with what he calls the "diabolical powers" of politics. We turn now to this work.

"POLITICS AS A VOCATION"

In the dismal, intentionally tedious first two-thirds of "Politics as a Vocation," Weber details the histories and effects of rationalization in modern politics, which yields bureaucratic and administrative mentalities, on the one hand, and party machines, with their bosses, hacks, and spoils, on the other.[27] He also charts the ways these party machines combine with the universal franchise to generate masses who are increasingly indifferent to reason and facts and thirsty for demagoguery. They cannot appreciate the complex internal and external relations of modern states and thus cannot be represented, only led. While a century earlier, aspiring political leaders might have employed a "style of rhetoric that addressed itself to reason," today they "make use of purely emotive language . . . to set the masses in motion." Plebiscitary democracy, Weber concludes, is the most that can now be hoped for and is properly described as "dictatorship based on the exploitation of the emotional nature of the masses."[28] It is a dismal picture, one that is intended to reveal why the realization of universal suffrage requires the reduction of democracy to its barest form.

Weber crafts his ideal political leader in relation to these conditions but in a mode that also aims to redeem grander possibilities for political life. It is a crafting drawn from a pre-bureaucratic, pre-rationalized past but is performed without sentimentality or nostalgia. The "heroic" quality of Weber's politician emerges precisely here, as a relation to the woeful contemporary conditions of politics and the effects of nihilism we have been considering. The sober political hero of modernity does not struggle against advancing armies or tyrants, but against bureaucratic torpor, party machinations, the stupidity of the masses, cynicism, defeatism, and the temptations of power stripped of connection to integrity, responsibility, vision, and purpose. The heroism rests in willingness to slog through this swamp while responsibly pursuing a serious and potentially history-altering political cause.

The inner qualities Weber identifies with a vocation for politics are well known. His ideal political leader is attracted to power but does not become intoxicated by it.[29] He is gratified by his capacity to influence people and history, but "daily and hourly" overcomes the temptations of vanity or narcissism.[30] He is relentlessly committed to realizing a worldview, but is neither egoistic nor obsessional and is humbled by consciousness that every cause is a matter of belief, not truth.[31] His power is rooted in charisma while his actions are contoured by restraint and far-sightedness. He is ethical in relation to concrete circumstances rather than principles that suspend or ignore context and the effects of actions, especially unintended ones.[32] He has the fortitude to stay the course amid endless setbacks and deep disappointments.[33] He resists cynicism, fatalism, and despair.

Each of these cultivated qualities or practices is a retort to the value depredations of rationalization and nihilism. Each centers worldly purpose, and eschews the gratifications of ego and cheap spectacle. Each crafts political desire as the wish to imprint one's vision on the world; each keeps cultivation of one's own power or reputation tightly leashed to this worldly purpose. Taken together, these qualities, and the tensions and overcomings they harbor, suggest there is nothing organic about Weber's figure of the ideal politician. It is not immanent to its conditions, though it must be savvy about them; rather, it is culled from a "calling" and rare inner resources. For this combination, Weber has only the limited vocabulary of "a cause" coupled with the "restraint," "fortitude," or "sobriety" to pursue the cause in a careful, responsible way. And while he tries to line up these qualities with charisma (about which more in a moment), sobriety, restraint, and perdurance are hardly charisma's most familiar features. Similarly, Weber draws on the secularized remnants of the Protestant ideal of serving God through earthly work, while doing away with the Almighty and substituting a compelling yet ultimately groundless *Weltanschauung* in its stead. Nor does Weber tether this figure to "authenticity," the craze for which in his time he deplored as weak, indulgent, or decadent, precisely opposite to the maturity, ascetic discipline, restraint, and confrontation with hard truths of the world that he sought to elevate.[34]

In short, Weber's politician is drawn from *Beruf* both secularized *and* constructed, a constructivism so obvious that he does not bother underlining it.[35] Arising neither from dialectics nor immanence, informed neither by social science nor religion, political possibility emerges from leaders bearing the spirit, force, and stamina to resist all the features of a nihilistic age with a passionate public purpose, responsibly pursued. This is Weber's wager: Not a revolutionary overthrow of the forces of the present (from which he feared only another machinery of domination) nor a capitulation to them (from which the plant of nihilism would grow only more robust). And no retreat from the political sphere to search for collective human meaning and value in spiritual or other existential domains. Rather, only responsible charismatic political leadership could renew, and redeem, the distinctly human capacity to shape or direct common life in accordance with the capacity to create value.

Why charisma? What are the elements of its internal temperament and external qualities about which we are so suspicious today, that Weber draws upon for working through or around nihilism in politics and political culture? In part, of course, Weber is seeking to exploit contemporary demands for demagoguery without surrendering to those demands, but instead re-orienting them. But there is more. Of the three kinds of authority Weber famously charts—charismatic, traditional, and rational-legal—only the first obtains obedience through challenging the givenness of the present, its powers and routines, its compass points and assumptions. Only charisma contests the forces and machineries dominating the present with an alternative vision. Only charisma challenges a disenchanted world with an alternative orbit of meaning. Charisma, on Weber's account, compels precisely through its disruption of the quotidian and the given, limning a something and somewhere else. It counters the nihilistic depression of value through both rejecting the fallen present and providing a vision that justifies that rejection. It counters the soullessness of institutionalized nihilism as well, as it draws away from institutionalization, administration, and routinization to reconnect political life with ideals and action.

Charismatic leadership is defined by the overwhelmingly attractive quality of the values the leader heralds or embodies, and a charismatic leader differs in this way from a mere demagogue. Revolutionary in a non-Marxist sense, charisma also challenges the value-depleting characteristics of rational-legal authority. It promises to re-enchant as it reforms the world. In Weber's account, charismatic leadership differs from other revolutionary modalities, not to mention garden-variety grandiosity, in its special balance of "inner determination" and "inner restraint," or what is sometimes translated as self-determination and self-limitation.[36] Charisma cannot be drawn from ego-distention without collapsing (the ego will cease to be a vehicle for the cause and instead become the cause), but it also cannot become formalized, regulated, or institutionalized without disappearing (the institutionalization will sacrifice the persona).[37]

Not only its requirements but much of charisma's force arises from this vital tension between passionate determination and restraint. Raw determination by itself easily corrupts or overwhelms the cause or becomes reckless ambition. Restraint alone veers toward moderation, compromise, or reluctance to act. But determination and restraint together, in tension, are the world-making force at the heart of charismatic leadership. This same tension will also be embodied in the distinctive ethic Weber formulates for political action. That ethic, which we will consider shortly, combines "heated passion and a cool sense of proportion" to achieve what he calls a "trained ruthlessness" toward one's cause (what some have called political Kantianism) and a "distance from people and things."[38]

Passion for a cause, restraint, determination, a sense of proportion, and a pathos of distance that Weber borrows from Nietzsche and transforms by divesting it of aristocratic airs and injecting it with asceticism—together these challenge the de-sublimated aggressions, petty preoccupations, rancorousness, self-absorption, and desire for immediate satisfaction of a nihilistic culture. These qualities also oppose what Weber takes to be other political motifs of the day—administrative, legalistic, or technocratic orientations, along with sensibilities he disparages as the "sterile excitement" of revolutionaries, the "naïve idealism" of purists and utopians, and the "frivolous intellectual play" of grandstanders and narcissists.[39]

Still, as I have already intimated, this fusion of Nietzsche with Kant, of a fierce power instinct and passion with egolessness and ascetic restraint, is awkward at best. Sober, dogged, responsible pursuit of an impersonal cause is not passion's quotidian form, especially in a nihilistic age, where "inner gravity" is in short supply and "windbags making themselves drunk on romantic sensations" are commonplace.[40] Thus the bearing and ethos Weber depicts requires routing passion away from its natural course, deferring or altogether denying its gratifications, and coloring it with "the habit of distance, in every sense of the word."[41] Weber has in this way constructed a nearly impossible figure: a charismatic personality with a strong instinct for power yet animated exclusively by care for the world, whose daily work is "a slow, powerful drilling through hard boards" and struggling against established machineries of power, and who is restrained, sober, detached, and consummately responsible.

Before we pursue this problem further, we need to ask, why does Weber reach for responsibility rather than reason as the harness for political passion? Especially since nihilism and demagoguery both cast reason in short supply? In an age dominated by instrumental rationality, reason alone only adds calculation or rationalization to any aim. Passion combined with instrumental reason leads to the most dangerous political tendency, in which ends justify means, and everything—laws, individuals, religions, principles—may be instrumentalized or degraded for purposes inimical to their original value. Not calculative reason, then, but a distinctive ethic of responsibility for *all* effects of an action, especially collateral and unintended ones, is required to guide and temporize without choking political passion.

In addition to avoiding instrumentalism, an ethic of responsibility is intended to curb vanity, "the deadly enemy of all dedication to a cause and of all distance . . . from oneself." Vanity, for Weber, stands for the moment when the political power instinct that is essential in any political actor overwhelms the cause to become "self-intoxication."[42] Vanity is also a name for identification with rather than distance from the imprint one is trying to make on history and from the power one wields for that aim. When a political actor *becomes* the cause rather than a vessel for it, reflexivity, detachment, restraint, and above all responsibility fall away, and the thrill of power takes center stage.

Weber dwells on the problem of vanity at length because he sees it not as merely an attribute of certain personalities, but endemic in politics, especially but not only when nihilism is in bloom. When "the demagogue is forced to play for 'effect' . . . he always runs the risk both of turning into an actor and of taking too lightly his responsibility for his own actions." Weber's judgment here is ferocious: "although, or rather because, power is an unavoidable tool of all politics, and the striving for power, therefore, is one of its driving forces, there is no more destructive distortion of political energy than when the *parvenu* swaggers around, boasting of his power, conceitedly reveling in its reflected glory." He damns the "impoverished and superficial indifference toward the *meaning* of human activity" embodied in this pose.[43] A pure expression of nihilism, its lack of commitment to anything other than itself and corresponding lack of responsibility comprise the "two kinds of mortal sin in the field of politics."[44]

Apart from the problem of vanity, Weber's argument for a distinctive political ethic of responsibility is conventionally read as a response to the unpredictable effects of action (what he calls "the tragedy of action" or the "ethical irrationality of politics") within a sphere suffused with "diabolical powers," including and especially violence.[45] As it twins alertness to power with depth of conviction, the ethic is Weber's formulation for navigating the Scylla and Charybdis of political life—pure *Machtpolitik* on one side, politics reduced to moral or ethical principles on the other. The argument is also aimed at contesting both rationalization and nihilism, the former's swallowing of freedom and greatness and the latter's reduction of politics to exercising power without right, violence without responsibility, thereby instrumentalizing and hence further deprecating value. Bound to leadership, the ethic of responsibility aims to re-center values, and politics as their province, after secularism shattered their foundation, rationalization destroyed their place, and nihilism destroyed their depth and dignity. This ethic is not only an individual holding, then, but is proffered by Weber as an *ethos* that could help recover politics as *the* domain of "struggle over ultimate values" while warding off the opposing dangers of weaponizing (hence degrading) values or conflating the political domain with the religious one. This ethos is essential to embedding values in the project of working through nihilism, both in individuals and society writ large. And it seeks to re-establish responsibility in the context of an ethically irrational order, in which what we aim to enact never remains in our control yet retains our authorship. Each of these post-nihilist strategies is worthy of closer examination.

Discussion of the ethic of responsibility comes near the end of "Politics as a Vocation," but is set up early. Weber opens the lecture by defining politics narrowly as leadership of a political organization ("in other words, a state") and then declares, curiously, that the modern state may be socio-logically stipulated only with reference to its peculiar means, namely its monopoly of physical violence.[46] Weber knows that there is more to states than this, and even more to its peculiar means; ensuing pages are dedi-cated to states' emergence and consolidation, their apparatuses and insti-tutions, and their distinctive organization of political life. He also identifies state ends with national glory. So why define states through their mono-poly of violence?

In part, Weber focuses on violence to set up his critiques of socialism, revolutionary Marxism, and Christian war pacificism. He believes that each of these doctrines, albeit in different ways, disingenuously and dan-gerously tends to isolate its formal virtues from its imbrication with vio-lence. More broadly, Weber is concerned with the wreckage unleashed when political ends are allowed to justify any means, a strong tendency in the age of instrumental rationality. Stipulating politics as state-centered and states as violence-centered thus importantly re-sutures the ultimate means of modern political life—state violence—to every political vision or project. This very re-suturing underscores both the intentional use of violence and its accidental unleashing as inescapable features of politics. Both hover over every political act and event, whether the aim is to lead, seize, or smash the state; prevent, start, join, or stop a war; initiate, re-form, or overturn a law. Again, Weber centers violence in his account of the political not to affirm it as the essence of politics—it is only an instru-ment, and the struggle over values is more important to him. Yet instru-ments are never "only" for this master theorist of the capacity of means to swallow ends. Thus he aims to throw on their feet and take the chair away from those who clutch their principles or defend their actions without reference to this instrument:

> Anyone who wishes to engage in politics at all . . . is entering into re-
> lations with the satanic powers that lurk in every act of violence. The
> great virtuosos of unworldly goodness and the love of humankind,
> whether from Nazareth or Assisi or the royal places of India, have
> never operated with the methods of politics, that is the use of force.
> Their kingdom was 'not of this world' and yet they were and are at
> work in this world. . . . Anyone who seeks the salvation of his soul
> and that of others does not seek it through politics, since politics
> faces quite different tasks, tasks that can only be accomplished with
> the use of force.[47]

More than warning against confusing righteous with political posi-
tioning, or religion with politics, Weber condemns concern with pure
principle in the political realm as a consequential category mistake. If the
political realm is suffused with *diabolical* power, that of organized human
violence, to pretend otherwise is not merely naïve but irresponsible. That
pretense, Weber knows, claims a good share of his audience. Disrupting it
is Weber's intellectual purpose with the ethic of responsibility he formulates as unique to politics. But his practical purpose is to burden actors with
responsibility for *both* means and ends while keeping them analytically
distinct. The same action or actor is responsible for both, and politics always comprises both. Thus neither abstract principle nor raw calculation

aimed at securing or enhancing one's power or cause have a place in a post-nihilist ethos or post-nihilist political action.

Weber famously contrasts an ethic of responsibility with two others. One he calls an "absolute ethic," which comprises conduct bound tightly to a moral code such as Christian virtue or principles of non-violence. Adherents to this ethic ignore the "tragedy of action," the intervals between motive, aim, and effect that Weber understands as comprising the ethical irrationality of the political realm, its failure to comport with a rational order in which intention dictates action and effect.[48] Relentless responsibility for consequences, especially unintended effects, is necessary precisely because of these intervals. It forbids "oops, I did not mean for that to happen" as an excuse for any effect of an action, intended or not. An absolute ethic, or what he sometimes terms "an ethic of conviction" does not so much rebut as disavow this dimension of politics. It also often, Weber says, decries a world "too stupid or too base" for one's principles to persuade or govern. Thus does an absolute ethic reveal itself as a form of *ressentiment* against politics.

The second foil for his ethic of responsibility, which Weber terms an "ethic of ultimate ends," refuses the ethical irrationality of politics very differently from the "absolute ethic." An ethic of ultimate ends is contoured not by principles but by its commitment to a rational ideal, one generally imagined devoid of distortions by power and partisanship. It is, in short, the problem of utopia. Because the ideal is rational (or beautiful, or perfect), any means to it may be considered justified by its adherents. Weber's main target here is Bolshevism. However, liberal politicians en-

gaged in imperial or colonial civilizational missions, and neoliberal politicians from Pinochet to Thatcher, are certainly vulnerable to this charge
as they justified state violence and other collateral damage to bring about
their ideal order.

Absolute-ethic political actors reduce political action to principles
while ultimate-ends political actors frame it in teleological or eschatolog-
ical terms. Both dangerously separate means from ends and eschew the
specific powers, partisanship, and "tragedy of action" that are permanent
features of politics. Both shirk responsibility for what becomes of their
actions and what they stand for. Moreover, if each hyper-personalizes the
ethical dimension of action, in the sense of referring everything back to
personal motive or aim, they also depersonalize the worldliness of action—its transformation in and by the world it intersects—and instead
treat principle or reason as governing action's meaning. This, too, avoids
responsibility in politics, the domain where purpose and effects so easily
come apart, where "the ultimate product of political activity frequently,
indeed, as a matter of course, fails utterly to do justice to its original purpose and may even be a travesty of it."[49]

Still, Weber famously concludes this discussion, only one who marries
an ethic of conviction to an ethic of responsibility truly has the vocation
for politics.[50] Only one who "feels the responsibility he bears for the consequences of his own action with his entire soul" yet is relentlessly committed to a cause can be a political hero.[51] So how are these ethics twinned
in a single being and set of practices? Weber's vocabulary here is telling:
maturity, sobriety, manly fortitude, restraint, and ability to withstand

crushing disappointment without whimpering, cynicism, or retreat.[52] The ability to persist "despite everything."[53] A "sense of proportion" in the pursuit of any political project.[54] Conversion of Nietzsche's complex "pathos of distance," from a class-based sensibility to generic "distance from self and things," a strange objectivity toward one's cause and its pursuit. This distance or objectivity keeps one bound to the cause and the force field in which one attempts to realize it, and quashes the temptation to satisfy oneself or others through postures or positions that are either irrelevant (righteous and otherworldly but also resentful) or reckless.

Still, there are moments when conviction will have to reign supreme, and Weber invokes Luther's resolute "here I stand, I can do no other" to express these occasions. Yet the invocation of Luther's famous phrase is somewhat misleading, as even here what is at stake is not virtue or saving one's own soul in the political realm, but such things as avoiding political complicity with sinister forces or exploiting circumstances in an effort to bring about something new. In these cases, some risk of unwanted or unknown effects may be worth the candle.[55] But Weber labors to avoid letting this be confused with an eruption of pure principle and the shrugging off of responsibility.

> I find it immeasurably moving when a mature human being—whether young or old in actual years is immaterial—who feels the responsibility he bears for the consequences of his own actions with his entire soul and who acts in harmony with an ethics of responsibility reaches the point where he says, 'Here I stand, I can do no other.'[56]

Where are we then? Weightiness, knowingness, tolerance for suffering rather than Nietzsche's gaiety and laughter for working through nihilism. Building rather than breaking things. Avoidance of resentment, egoism, vengeance, even ordinary face-saving—all the reactive and vain temptations. Above all, the ethic of the post-nihilist political actor entails a sacrifice of self but not others to a vision, and steadfastly refuses nihilistic reductions of political life to individual interest, advantage, power, or security. However, the ethic of responsibility also represents a path through nihilism in its paradoxical representation of the nature of "ultimate value" in political life and by inhabiting a set of difficult political epistemological commitments to renew human freedom. Let us consider this epistemological politics more closely.

To take one's own values as True is already to inhabit something of the absolute ethic Weber criticizes. Conversely, recognizing one's political values as sincere beliefs abets the pathos of distance Weber seeks in responsible action. In a sphere that is partisan all the way down, this paradoxical affirmation of the contingency of the ultimate values for which one is fighting builds the sense of proportion that in turn builds responsibility at the site of conviction. Thus, Weber might be seen as adapting one of Nietzsche's signature moves, in which rejecting both the disembodied conceits of science and the absolutism of religion is crucial to reconstructing objectivity and its grounds. For Nietzsche, only perspectivism permits the possibility of interpretation beyond the interpreter, only affirmation of affect permits reflexivity in knowing, and only multiplication of perspectives and affects permits an approximation of objectivity. ("There is

only a perspective seeing, only a perspective 'knowing'; and the more affects we allow to speak about one thing, the more eyes, different eyes, we
can use to observe one thing, the more complete will our 'concept' of this
thing, our 'objectivity,' be."[57]) For Weber, only reckoning with the founda-
tionless and irreconcilable quality of ultimate values retrieves them from
nihilistic devaluation, with its destructive effects of instrumentalization,
trivialization, and hyper-politicization of values.

Put the other way around, the ethic of responsibility entails acting
without the conceit that history and humanity have a natural or necessary ethical shape or teleology, or unfold from pure intention, reason, or
religion. The ethic both circumscribes and affirms politics as the domain
where value is articulated, fought for *and* transformed by context rather
than a place where pristine value is realized. An ethic of conviction and
an ethic of ultimate ends both refuse this, which is why each is irresponsible, as well as irrelevant to politics.

That said, Weber's ethic makes an incredible demand on what he takes
to be the vanishing human soul in the age of rationalization. As he demands our unblinking consciousness of the contingent nature of our convictions and of the enormous obstacles to their realization, he also demands our complete dedication to them, resting our humanity and our
freedom on this dedication. Only in this form can the struggle over values
mend the desire that nihilism has broken *and* avoid the decadence, irresponsibility, and presentism that nihilistic conditions incite. To be clear,
this practice of reflexivity, responsibility, and restraint tethered to passion
has nothing to do with relativism, subjectivism, or climbing "empathy

walls." Rather, it is an unprecedented epistemological-political conscious-ness, in which one knows one's values to be both situated and partial tem-porally, geographically, and spiritually, yet is no less committed to them by virtue of that consciousness. This post-nihilist affirmation of the complex nature of political struggle—from the contingent nature of one's passionate political attachments to the violence with which the struggle for them is implicated and for which one must be responsible, to the need for pa-tience and endurance in struggling for one's cause—is what the terms "sobriety," "maturity," "heroism," and "manliness" carry for Weber.

Consciousness of the ethical irrationality of political life formed by the tragedy of action, the rationalities governing the present, *and* the episte-mological undecidability of values in a secular age also places political predicaments, political possibilities, and political perils in a distinctive light. These become differently legible for scholars when they cease to be measured by moral or behavioral logics abstracted from historical condi-tions and contingent attachments, and for actors when they are detached from both moral Manicheanism and pure power politics.[58] The ethic Weber prescribes also aims to retrieve political life from its overtaking by personality cults and a spirit of *ressentiment* on one side, and bureaucrati-zation and rationalization on the other. This in turn creates the possi-bility of bids for the future that are not rooted in grievances (against the past or present) or in a nihilistic attachment to the personal and the immediate.

Finally, Weber's approach to political renewal aims to recuperate *freedom* from its destruction by rationalization and from its nihilistic

49

descent into irresponsible license or weaponry against the social fabric. To understand this recuperation, we must appreciate that Weber offers two quite different meanings and practices of freedom across his work. In his social science typologies of action and rationality, Weber defines freedom in a relatively mechanical liberal frame as the absence of constraints on action. Instrumental rationality, for example, is freer than other kinds because it is not bound by moral constraints. Elsewhere, however, Weber insists that freedom's wellspring is "the soul," that it involves enacting a life we have chosen and living by the lights of our beliefs, in short, governing and, through that, realizing the self. It is this second meaning that leads Weber to align *Beruf* with freedom, even to place it at freedom's heart. When we live according to what we consciously value or feel called by, we are in a certain way living freely, even amid difficult or constraining conditions.

Nihilism, generated in part by the expanded force and venue of freedom's mechanical form (the throwing off of religious and traditional authority, the rise of instrumental rationality), threatens to extinguish freedom's soulful form. This is the story Weber tells of capitalism, industrialization, and bureaucracy, of disenchantment and ubiquitous rationalization, which together culminate in the "iron cage" that houses us all in modernity.[59] The iron cage, unrelated to state carceral power, is no less devitalizing for freedom. Its distinctiveness rests not only in its production through forms of rationality or its universal reach, but in the fact that it is crafted by the accidental effects of one form of freedom, which destroys another. Just as rationalization trammels inner freedom with instrumental calculation, so also do economic and administrative systems that originate as mere "means" eventually invert freedom into its opposite. More than just different, the two forms of freedom are mutually cancelling. Freedom as unconstrained power builds an order in which we are, subjectively and practically, largely bereft of the freedom to craft ourselves and the world according to values we choose or at least affirm, individually or collectively.

Weber's bold bid in "Politics as a Vocation" is to task the heroic leader with resisting the forces destroying inner freedom and value rationality, and thus recuperate politics itself from the nihilistic dynamics plaguing it in his time and overrunning it in ours. By placing the struggle for a passionately held political vision at the heart of the political vocation, and placing the vocation for politics at the vanguard of resistance to its rationalization and nihilistic degradation, Weber invests the politician with more than responsible leadership in action. Rather, this figure carries the hope of rescuing humanity itself from the forces with which it is destroying its capacity to make worlds in accord with consciously chosen values. This figure also rescues freedom from erasure by machineries of capitalism and administration (institutional nihilism) and soulless yet narcissistic power plays (personal nihilism). If contemporary politics is saturated with both, indeed, if Weber's greatest dread was giant apparatuses of domination wielded by vain, narcissistic demagogues, politics also remained the place where both could be countered.

Weber's lecture on politics as a vocation is itself a practice of working through nihilism by restoring politics to its ancient meaning—the struggle over "who we are" and "what we should do"—while accepting the explicitly contemporary quality of this struggle.[60] It aims to make politics redemptive after the death of God, not by cleansing it of diabolical powers but by reasserting the value of values in political life against its modernist predicaments there. In doing so, Weber also renders politics the place where humans could become responsible again, not only for their own actions but for the world when this capacity is imperiled, on the one hand, by humanly generated powers that have slipped our control—those of capital, technology, and organized political violence—and, on the other hand, by nihilism's reduction of politics to raw power play. Weber presses against both so that human purposes and responsibility might retake the world. Could anything be more important today, when the powers we have generated but do not steer threaten not merely to dominate but to finish us, along with all other earthly life?

If Weber was alert to the faint prospects for this project, the antidote to despair was not hope but grit—emotional, spiritual, and practical. This character demand is not limited to political leaders but extended to anyone who cares about political life, justice, or futurity. Most of us, he says, are "occasional politicians," that is, interested in politics or moved to participate in some debates or campaigns, and his final sentences are addressed to those who are "neither a leader nor a hero" but still must "arm themselves with the staunchness of heart that refuses to be daunted by the collapse of all their hopes." Only those whose "spirit will not be broken if the world . . . proves too stupid or base to accept what he wishes to offer it, and who . . . can still say "Nevertheless! despite everything"—only they are fit for politics.[61] "Nevertheless" or "in spite of it all" does not leap over the nihilistic predicament but resists its world-eviscerating force with seriousness, integrity, endurance, and responsible handling of power in pursuit of a world-changing cause. We could not be further from Nietzsche now.

WEBER FOR THE LEFT

Charismatic leadership tends to worry, if not repel, left and liberal thinkers. There is radical democratic anxiety about leadership as an inevitably hierarchical formation. There is liberal democratic anxiety about its potential usurpation of representation. There is Habermasian anxiety about surrendering reason as the source of political agency and mobilization. There is widely shared anxiety about the dangers of despotism that charismatic leadership portends, fear that flirtation with such leadership breeds or legitimates unchecked power. Consequently, many progressives denounce left populism today, and not only Leninism of old. Others defend leaderless social movements, uprisings without clear or consolidated demands, or horizontalism and sociocracy.[62]

These anxieties about charismatic leaders may be taken seriously without allowing them to govern. Charisma, with its capacity to incite and excite, inspire and mobilize, and above all lead beyond business as usual, is an indisputably potent element of political life. For the Left to do without it while the Right milks it for advantage is to ensure defeat while hewing to the kind of virtuous political ethos that Weber warns against. Liberal centrists, in particular, at times seem prepared for the world to go up in flames while clutching institutions, proceduralism, reason, and civility. The mistake here is more than pragmatic or strategic, however. Rejection of charismatic leadership misunderstands both politics and reason in the effort to preserve modernity's peculiar promise of freedom based on their conjoining. It imagines political arguments free of rhetorical power, prevailing only on the basis of their evidentiary and logical soundness. It imagines reason in an abstract and autonomous register, independent of cultural location, forms of rationality, and their particular terms of discourse. Above all, it imagines reason as independent of desire, if not opposed to it.

These are consequential misunderstandings. Among other things, they anoint the Left with rationality and tar the Right exclusively with false consciousness or bad faith—greed, supremacisms, or ambition for power parading as justice and right. In this, they reproduce the intellectual disdain that many drawn to the Right chafe against and that right-wing politicians exploit. They also align a left value constellation with truth, disavowing the ardor, rancor, will to power, and historical contingency in this constellation. Moreover, in mistaking the political theater for an academic debating hall, the Left shrinks from crafting its own passionate attachments as a compelling future and grasping in order to wound, exploit, or co-opt the passions of its enemy. Instead, the left rationalists are limited to calling out hypocrisies and fictions in right-wing projects or exposing their nefarious funding streams or networks. Always on its back foot in this regard, the Left is perplexed by its own failures and shrinking ground as its enemies today flirt ever more openly with authoritarianism and fascism.

The point is not that the Left should learn to play dirty. Or substitute emotion for thoughtful and informed argument, lies for truth, convenient fictions for science. Or hew to Sorelian irrationalism and blind belief in myth. All of this would deepen nihilism and hasten the end of democracy, and miss the opportunity to challenge the binaries contributing to predicaments of the present. Rather, the point is that we need to surrender the opposition between reason and desire in the political sphere, along with conceits that reason could ever defeat desire in politics, or that conceptual philosophical refinements or science solve political problems. Above all we need to surrender every variation on the notion that only false consciousness keeps the masses from knowing and acting on their true interests in equality and emancipation. Often the masses want neither; their desires run another way, and the challenge is to harness and reroute these desires. Desire is not infinitely malleable, but if it is understood and gratified with recognition, it can be crafted and redirected.

Our task is to incorporate concern with desire into political thinking, action, and persuasion at every turn, whether we are analyzing climate denialism and opposition to abortion or fashioning a campaign designed to traverse hardened political polarities. How might we mobilize the desire to live comfortably for building an order that supports rather than imperils life, both human and non-human? How might we mobilize care for innocent life for protecting vulnerable life of every kind? How might we mobilize the longing for respect and belonging for resistance to ubiquitous powers of subordination, humiliation, and abjection?

Attention to political desire draws us near an orbit of thinkers on the Left—Sorel, Gramsci, Marcuse, Stuart Hall, among others—who looked to culture and feeling to replace and supplement economism, spontaneity, and reason as sources of revolutionary enthusiasm among the masses. This kind of thinking, of course, is far from Weber's own heart, especially but not only the Sorelian strain that fetishized violence and valorized mythos over logos. Yet Weber's particular formulation of charismatic leadership may be precisely what is needed to make this tradition more responsible, compelling, and relevant to the present. Only charismatic political leadership, Weber insisted, could productively re-enchant the political realm, disrupting its machineries of domination with visions and forms of action redemptive of the human power to shape the world. Grounded in inner discipline and restraint, charismatic leadership tethered to relentless responsibility for event-chains in the singular theater of politics both leads to and models a way of linking revolutionary ardor for another world with concern for life in this one. Far from acting from impulse or instinct, let alone vanity or belief in the superior ethical worth of a cause, Weber's hero disrupts the status quo through close respect for its powers and coordinates while doggedly pursuing paths to new ones. This figure holds out revolutionary hope that comports with neither myth nor utopia while breaking the open closures of the present.

For Weber, sober, responsible, purposive leadership in the contemporary political realm includes appreciating the extraordinary difficulty of resisting, let alone overcoming, forms of rationality and rationalization that govern to bring about alternatives; recognizing violence as the ultimate means, and power as the only currency of the realm; consciousness of the contingent nature of one's cause along with the distance between intentions and effects; and commitment to awakening human longing for something to believe in and hope for. These are also indispensable elements of a left politics, and their combination is especially important in turning aside fatalism and resisting nihilism. While we have been focused on their embodiment in leadership, this very embodiment can also be a form of political education. Leaders who are passionate *and* responsible, visionary *and* careful, inspirational *and* sober, hold lessons for social movements and citizenries alike.

This said, political education, and its complex entwinement with desire, cannot be left to the political realm alone. If Weber is right that political worldviews, "values," emerge from complex attachments and desires, and if nihilism represents a crisis of desire, an impasse in loving this life and this world, then education of feeling or attachment becomes fundamental to building a post-nihilist future. This education becomes all-important as we abandon the conceit that our values are true and those of our opponents false, that political values are a matter of discovery rather than legislation, and that either reason or interests will naturally counter seduction by authoritarianism or chicanery, by unsustainable supremacies of species, race, or gender, or by nihilistic versions of freedom (nihilistic because they do not serve life in any sense). Weber's position, a retort to liberals and Marxists alike, reminds us that rational argument and compelling evidence by itself does not counter popular fears and frustrations, attachments and yearnings. Rather, the task of those invested in a more just and sustainable order is to kindle and educate *desire* for such an order and to build that desire into a worldview and viable political project.[63]

So we began with the problem of nihilism and political action and end with the problem of education, a problem that takes us toward Weber's other Vocation Lecture, on knowledge. As the next chapter will make clear, for Weber, analyzing values and their entailments in an intellectually serious way, which is one task he assigns to social science scholars, is a vital prophylactic against the nihilistic degradation of knowledge into purely instrumental and power purposes. To be sure, Weber will approach this project strangely and unsatisfyingly—after identifying values as constellations of passionate attachments, he will insist on submitting them to the scrutiny of cool reason. Nevertheless, his thinking will provide a productive reframing for contemporary struggles over the problem of values in classrooms, curriculums, and pedagogy today. It will also help us reflect on the broader predicaments of higher education. If nihilism devalues all value, including the value of truth, facticity, history, and theory, this effect converges with and is exploited by neoliberal diminution of all forms of thought or knowledge irrelevant to capital enhancement. It is ramified as well by the powers of unaccountable media and right-wing attacks on intellectualism. As these forces together erode the quality, accessibility, and the very worth of education apart from skill development, one result is the manipulable, undemocratic populations that have brought democracy itself into crisis.

Weber responded to crises of European politics in his time by giving up on substantive democracy and investing (faint) hope in responsible charismatic leadership, where responsibility embodies "politics of the head," and charisma captures the ineffable capacity to move the soul and the passions. However, the unbridgeable moat he built and policed between the academic and the political realm, and between truth and power, deepened the prospects for something else, namely irresponsible demagogues crassly preying on popular fears, suffering, wounded supremacism, and scapegoating, themselves unchecked by accountability to facts, law, constitutions, institutions, humanity, or ecosystems. Confining the academy to scientific reason and politics to responsibilized passion, Weber argued for divorcing these realms to protect them from each other. As we shall see, these moves diminished the prospects of educating for democracy, including educating desire, that could prevent what he most dreaded: excited masses mobilized by irresponsible demagogues in charge of enormous state and economic machineries, and often clamoring for war.[64] At the same time, Weber's corridors of separation sharply curtail academic contributions to the project of repairing political, economic, and social life.[65] In "Science as a Vocation," to which we now turn, Weber struggled so fiercely to preserve knowledge production and dissemination from nihilistic politicization that he radically attenuated their potential contribution to transforming the world, or even holding back the dark.

TWO | KNOWLEDGE

Positively affirming the value of science is the *precondition* of all teaching.
—MAX WEBER

Science is meaningless because it has no answer to the only questions that matter to us: "What should we do? How shall we live?"
—MAX WEBER, quoting Tolstoy

Weber's ontological politics, populated with the furious struggles of gods and demons, and so incongruous in the thought of a founder of the scientific study of society and politics, issue from the frustration of a consciousness that knows that its deepest values are owed to religion but that its vocational commitments are to the enemy.
—SHELDON S. WOLIN

NIHILISM IN THE ACADEMY

The previous chapter explored Weber's effort to counter nihilistic effects in and on politics, especially through political action animated by responsible, selfless pursuit of a public cause. We turn now to Weber's efforts, in "Science as a Vocation," to resist nihilistic effects on knowledge and in the academy, a project that relies on arch depoliticization and secularization of scholarship, and a project that ultimately fails both because such purism is impossible and because even as it resists certain nihilistic effects, it intensifies others. Both the effort and the failure, however, are fecund for contemporary thinking about post-nihilist knowledge politics, which is how we shall approach Weber's lecture.

"Science as a Vocation" is well known for drawing a dark line between facts and values and for reprimanding both those who mix them and those who openly advance values, especially but not only their embodiment in political positions or programs in academic settings. However, far from excising values from scholarly consideration, Weber argues for analyzing them as ethical and political constellations with entailments for action, power, and violence. So important is this matter that in the portion of the lecture concerning ethical pedagogy, Weber turns not to the question of how to teach facts (its own challenge given his hermeneutic commitments) but of how to handle values in the classroom. If what he calls "ultimate values" exceed mere personal beliefs contouring individual lives to shape political causes imbricated with that realm's "diabolical powers," then they must be withdrawn from the moral or theological castles in which they are often locked and submitted to rigorous analysis of their premises, "internal structure," and entailments.[1]

Such an approach differs radically from contemporary bids for teachers to "balance" political views with opposing ones, or to let them "compete" with one another for attractiveness, or to crown some political value systems as moral or correct while denouncing others as evil or wrong. These approaches leave values unexamined, implicitly rendering them as beyond the ken of the classroom, either because they are sacred and hence untouchable, or because they are mere opinion and hence unimportant, or because they are subjective and hence unscientific. Each turns them into objects of deference or derision rather than of beady-eyed analysis.

Weber, by contrast, treats values as emerging from *Weltanschauungs* without rational origins or ultimate foundations, yet no less analyzable for that. Moreover, treating values in scholarly fashion is all important in a scientific age that both threatens value and confuses us about its status. The paradox of the "irrational" origin, content, and play of value, and a commitment to rationally analyzing it, is a vital dimension of what makes his perspective useful today. Weber implores scholars, especially but not only in their teaching capacity, to approach contemporary value concatenation "scientifically" even though the origins of values and the ultimate domain for their contestation lie in nonscientific domains—feeling or attachment for the former and politics for the latter. His wager is that academic commitment to cool and impartial deconstruction of values can be a scene of sober mediation between these two, that is, between the subjective and political realms, but only if subjectivity and politics are both barred from the academy. This paradox comprises the very scene of knowledge and the classroom that Weber aims to theorize, circumscribe, and protect.

Weber is adamant that philosophers, theologians, or social scientists cannot and should not solve value disputes. The scholar's task, and the ethical requirement of a pedagogue, is to treat values as objects of analysis and critique—that is, to examine them through historical and comparative analysis or through consideration of their logics and entailments, but not as matters of truth. We teachers can illuminate the stakes, implications, and possible trajectories of values in practice; we can help students clarify the meaning and entailments of the positions they hold. We cannot settle which values are right. This said, securing a dispassionate and thoughtful domain for analyzing value clashes may render their clashes—in an age of value proliferation and deracination, a secular and increasingly nihilistic age—both more substantive and less strident. Such scholarly and pedagogical work thus has potential for indirectly enriching the public sphere, and at the same time for burnishing the integrity and reputation of the academy. At a time when both domains are in peril and disrepute, this would be no minor accomplishment.

As we begin consideration of Weber's account of the scholarly vocation, it is important to remember that *Wissenschaft,* routinely translated into English as "science," refers to all systematic academic study, not only the natural or physical sciences.[2] At the core of the Humboldtian model of education, *Wissenschaft* in Weber's time bore implications of knowledge pursuit that was internally unbiased *and* independent of external influence, especially by church and state. Knowledge is capable of being true, the assumption goes, only when this neutrality and autonomy prevail. This is the complex meaning-bundle at stake each time we encounter the term "science" in Weber's lecture. I hasten to add, however, that while Weber drew on the (fading) Humboldtian commitment to intellectual freedom as unveiling the factual world, he rejected the exalted moral and national purpose that Humboldt ascribed to scholarly endeavor and to universities.[3] Weber codifies the value of both as importantly divorced from such purpose and stipulates the value of *Wissenschaft* more narrowly.

RESISTING POLITICIZATION

As with the lecture on politics, Weber opens "Science as a Vocation" with a discussion of contemporary conditions for the vocation that he was invited to reflect upon. With a focus on contemporary German academic life, he paints these conditions in dismal hues. There is its feudal organization and reward structure that yield both low standards for teaching and the failure to reward excellent scholarship. There is the precariousness of much academic labor. There are the confines of steadily growing scholarly specialization and the inevitable eclipse of every achievement by scientific progress. Above all, there is science's own disenchantment of the world. With its promise that we can, in principle, understand the workings of everything, science bleeds spirit from its objects, depleting what it studies not only of mystery but of intrinsic value or meaning. In its way, it is as violent as politics, as desacralizing as capitalist commodification, as eviscerating of value as instrumental reason. In its way, *Wissenschaft* violates, desacralizes, or eviscerates not peoples, nations, vocations, and relations but meaning and value themselves. It rationalizes whatever it touches, toppling miracle, reverence, and faith and putting dissection, price, or function in their place. It divorces progress from its millenarian promise of improvement, emancipation, or happiness and reduces it to accumulation of knowledge and technique. It leaves the world more suffused with power and depleted of meaning than it finds it.

Such is the condition Weber believes we face consequent to the dethronement of religious authority and mysteries of nature by science. As it topples religious and theological accounts of order and meaning, science cannot replace what it destroys. The inclination to do so, more than merely misguided, is itself a dangerous nihilistic effect: the voids opened in a radically desacralized world create a demand, Weber says, for prophets and demagogues everywhere, and for ideas that excite and incite. Performances in the realm of knowledge that belong in the church and political sphere become part of nihilism's destructive force in which, as Weber formulates the matter, "the ultimate and most sublime values have withdrawn from public life," and theology, with its inescapable "assumption that the world must have a meaning," is finished.[4] This nihilistic force, and the demands that emerge from it, are an important part of what Weber wrestles with in this lecture.

However, Weber's concern is not only with these world-historical forces, but with attitudes toward them and misapprehensions about them. In "Science as a Vocation" and his earlier essays on method from which much of the lecture's argument is built, Weber is at war. He is at war with Marx and Nietzsche for the soul of the social sciences, contesting what he regards as the norm-laden faux science of Marx and the anti-science of Nietzsche. He is at war with romantics who fetishize the irrational or make a new religion out of everyday life or "authenticity." He is at war with academic colleagues who promote German nationalism from their scholarly podiums, with colleagues who are value positivists and colleagues who are syndicalists. (The nationalists make the university "into a theological seminary—except that it [lacks] the latter's religious dignity." The positivists make a category error, refusing the Kantian dictum to submit everything to critical scrutiny, eschewing the interpretive dimension of understanding action and values, and reifying the coordinates and norms of the present. The syndicalists both spurn objectivity and exploit the power of the academic podium in the manifestly inegalitarian classroom setting.[5]) Weber is at war with those who believe truth rests in balancing or achieving compromise between contesting views, a technique appropriate to politics, not science—when it infiltrates the latter, it relativizes facticity and trivializes ultimate worldviews, a relativization and trivialization expressive of nihilism.[6] He is at war with those who would submit diverse views to competition, a technique appropriate to markets, not science—when it infiltrates the latter, it indexes the invasion of the university by market values.[7] He is at war with those who pretend "the facts speak for themselves" when facts do not speak at all, when this likely means that both matters of interpretation and "inconvenient facts" are being strategically ignored, moves that also bring rhetorical sleights of hand appropriate to political debate into the classroom.[8] He is at war with those who believe they have achieved neutrality by structuring their historical or sociological accounts with *realpolitik,* with Darwinian adaptation, or with metanarratives of progress—each is an ungrounded theological remainder inappropriate to scholarly objectivity.[9] He is at war with economists who believe their science establishes the normative supremacy of capitalism when it can never do more than describe its mechanisms and dynamics.[10] He is at war with philosophers and social theorists who believe they can assess, let alone certify, the validity of norms, rather than merely analyze their predicates, logics, and implications. And he is at war with those who believe in transcendental reason, who acknowledge neither the inescapability of hermeneutics nor differing modes of rationality within which there are always irrationalities.

Weber is at war, but his enemies are not timeless stalwarts. Rather, he understands most of what he is fighting as effects of political, epistemological, and existential conditions of his time. He takes his moral-political age to be one simultaneously drained of value, proliferating value, and cheapening value, one in which value judgments are frequently reduced to matters of taste, one that features false prophets in the absence of real ones, one that venerates personality in place of integrity and honesty, and one that promulgates freedom as license within unprecedented orders of domination. In an age he famously depicted as featuring "sensualists without heart" and "specialists without spirit," neither feeling nor intellect are preserved from the rationalization that simultaneously renders us cogs in economic machineries and superficial individualists.[11] Truth has come apart from Meaning and Value to reside only in facts. Facts in turn are both infinite in number and always interpreted, a humbling as well as daunting reality that, when not accepted, produces reaction in the form of polemics, positivism, sectarianism, and millenarianism in the knowledge domain. Progress no longer promises growing happiness, peace, or truth; it is limited to advancements of knowledge and techniques that paradoxically generate conditions for greater domination rather than greater freedom. As the organizational, technological, economic, and political machineries built from these advancements escape human control, they become world-blistering forces of power without right.

Boundary breakdown is also a key symptom of the age. Nothing stays in its place because, absent a moral lodestar and the organizing principles secured by tradition, place itself loses both its naturalized coordinates and its value. In the domain of knowledge, the incessant mixing of what Weber refers to repeatedly as "absolutely heterogeneous" practices— most notably analyses of facts and value judgments about them—degrades each, intensifying cynical disregard for facts, truth, accountability, responsibility, *and* values. Thus does nihilism ramify as it corrodes boundaries between preaching and teaching, entertainment and information, personality and politics. Depth, sobriety, historical consciousness, and care for souls and the world give way to superficiality, instrumentality, excitability, personal gratification, presentism.

Weber responds to this crisis and the spiraling miscegenation of elements it foments with his infamous stipulation of opposites and an epistemological and ontological hygiene aimed at isolating and insulating these opposites from each other. The familiar binaries he asserts are politics and knowledge, the classroom and the public square, fact and value, empirical and theoretical claims, positive descriptions and normative judgments.[12] Importantly, for Weber, not method alone but the world is at stake in drawing and enforcing these separations. If the relative organicism of earlier epochs has given way to fragmentation and specialization in the age of capitalism, bureaucracy, and secularism, this means order once secured by hierarchy and authority has given way to life cleaved by value concatenation and dominated by "inanimate machineries." With both organicism and authority receding, tightly enforced organization is all that remains to secure order. Notwithstanding Weber's sensitivity to what he calls the "chaos of infinitely differentiated and contradictory complexes of ideas and feelings" in any epoch or ideational regime, and notwithstanding his admonition to scholars to avoid conflating concepts and typologies with reality, Weber's way through nihilism in the intellectual sphere depends on fierce epistemological-ontological distinctions. More than establishing conceptual tidiness, these distinctions are sent into the field as police.[13]

Why? Why formulate these "absolutely heterogeneous" spheres of endeavor and practice—knowledge / politics, facts / values, truth / judgment—not as merely expressive of modal differences but as opposites that destroy each other when they touch or mix? Weber's adamancy on this front aims at quarantining nihilistic effects in the academy, those ranging from the destruction of truth (reduced to empirical knowledge but at risk there too), to the final destruction of meaning (reduced to "ultimate values" but at risk there too), to the destruction of scholarly greatness (reduced to a cause for which the scholar is a vessel). Only by insulating the certainty of facticity from the undecidability of values can the nihilistic condition assaulting and degrading both be repelled. When students crave meaning and ultimate values in a world of moral chaos, only by insulating teaching from charisma can the classroom "unlock the world by means of the intellect."[14] And, paradoxically, only by imposing unbridgeable moats between church, politics, and the academy can the order they formerly secured by their entwinement be stabilized in the wake of their fragmentation.

Weber's protocols, then, do not simply shed the fetters of a less scientific era but address nihilism's world-destroying de-sublimations and boundary breakdowns with a program of hygiene. These protocols aim at challenging value warriors and politicians of every stripe who bend facticity to their cause to the point of breaking it. They challenge journalists and teachers who practice faux objectivity while being manifestly partisan as they frame, select, and arrange facts. They challenge the conceit that neutrality is obtained by balancing or synthesizing views—through competition, or through finding middle ground.[15] They seek to preserve truth by confining it to facts and preserve value by assigning it to politics where its undecidability and contested character is on permanent and vivid display. And they challenge teachers, and not only scholars, to lock away their personal passions and personalities while doing their work.

Since Weber is conventionally understood as codifying protocols of value-neutral social science for a secular age, it is worth examining more closely the specific crisis for knowledge that he aims to redress with his category purifications. What has vanished in recent decades, Weber writes in his 1917 essay, "The Meaning of Ethical Neutrality," is "the widespread conviction among social science scholars that of the various possible points of view in the domain of practical-political preferences, ultimately only one was the correct one."[16] In its stead, he continues, "a patchwork of cultural values *and personalities*" to advance them have replaced the "relatively impersonal" because supra-personal character of the old ethical imperative.[17] In addition to value proliferation, Truth's dethronement in morals and politics elevates the individual and personality as carriers of values. This is part of what generates the widespread demand for demagoguery everywhere—church, state, classroom.[18] For Weber, fusing value promulgation with personality is especially dangerous in the domain of knowledge: as facticity wobbles along with ethical monoculture, the political partisan and the preacher invade the classroom dressed in professorial garb. The same historical conditions necessitating pristine scholarly integrity—respect for facts and an approach to values only as analytic objects—undermine it by feeding the rise of personality. That cult of personality, Weber suggests, is one that students crave and unethical teachers gratify.[19] It is intensified in our time by the loop between a ubiquitous culture of celebrity that reaches into academic life itself, reliance on students to evaluate pedagogy, and the growing dependence of marketized universities on student satisfaction. The quiet purveyors of methodologically certified knowledge for which Weber argues cannot easily buck, or survive, these trends and practices.

The classroom, Weber insists, is for training, not molding students; developing intellectual capacities, not inculcating worldviews.[20] This means teaching the importance of "inconvenient facts" (including those that unsettle worldviews or narratives to which we hew), distinguishing facts from evaluations and judgments of them, and disciplining students to "repress the impulse to exhibit [their own] personal tastes or sentiments" in their studies. They must be taught that intellectual greatness rests in training, discipline, industry, specialization, devotion, and restraint of ego investment—all the familiar Protestant virtues bundled into the scholarly vocation.[21] These virtues, Weber hoped, would not simply harness but choke the will to power that has no place in intellectual life, although, as Nietzsche and Freud understood, that life force must go somewhere, and we will see its emergence later on.[22] Weber also knows that these demands aggrandize precisely the ascetic forces—objectivism, neutrality, dispassion, denial of the subject of knowing—that Nietzsche grasped as turning us against our senses, bodies, historicity, faculties of interpretation, and will to truth. Weber's project for the scholar, then, chases nihilism from one door while letting it in through another.

Weber tries but fails to twist away from Nietzschean conclusions. The pointlessness of dedication to accumulating knowledge, which risks going unrecognized and is certain to be superseded, is a leitmotif of his lecture. The frustration and ennui of the modern scholar is repeatedly acknowledged and never resolved. To the contrary Weber insists that knowledge confined to what can be empirically established and neutrally analyzed requires that "the human element" in the drive to know be objectivized rather than unleashed. He calls for knowledge practices that not only starve the knower of gratification and starve the world of meaning but turn the will to know (or the will to power in knowing) against its own source, lashing it with unparalleled ferocity due to its close containment. This turning of the self against the self, Nietzsche insisted, would reach a crescendo in Western civilization where we would come to will nothingness even as we broke into decadence—two loud symptoms of nihilism in political culture today. What is refusal to stem climate change and affirmation of being governed by markets rather than humans other than the will to nothingness? What is the festive spurning of facts and truth by power without right other than decadence? What is open destruction of democratic norms and institutions in order to salvage power for an eroding demographic base other than pure power politics, itself an outgrowth of nihilism?

VALUES

As I have already suggested, notwithstanding Weber's insistence that science dwells exclusively in facts, his fiercest and finest moments in "Science as a Vocation" pertain to how scholars and teachers ought to analyze values. Why? In the previous essay I argued that Weber identifies values with politics, and politics with partisanship, power, force, and, at the extreme, violence. This chain of identifications is shorthand for a historical process Weber charts that bears significantly on the problem of handling values academically in a nihilistic age. In one of his earlier methodological essays, Weber identifies values not with politics but culture.[23] To be cultural creatures, Weber says, is to be "endowed with the capacity and the will to take a deliberate attitude towards the world and to lend it *significance*."[24] The very concept of culture, he adds, is a "value concept . . . empirical reality becomes 'culture' to us because and insofar as we relate it to value ideas."[25] (We don't merely eat, procreate, and learn, but enjoy cuisines, build institutions like families, and develop curriculums reflecting who "we" take ourselves to be.) How, then, do values shift from the cultural to the political plane in late modernity? Values become political in Weber's terms when they are deracinated, detached from an authoritative worldview that is both grounded and shared. At this point, they become matters of struggle, undecidable except (provisionally) by rhetorical, legal, or physical force. As we have seen, this is also when they become vulnerable to nihilistic hyper-politicization. The politicization of culture, arising from value uprooted from foundations and detached from authority, is part of what makes liberalism itself crack: multiculturalism in the broadest sense only works when culture remains depoliticized, a depoliticization possible only when value is both anchored and common. What we call the age of identity politics did not change all this but is, rather, the measure of its loss.[26]

The chain of distinctly contemporary identifications Weber establishes between values, politics, partisanship, and force does three consequential things. First, it converts all values into practical positions available to cool analysis and situates their worldly enactment in a realm where the disjunction between motives and effects demands responsibility to that disjunction rather than to principles alone. No religious or other moral raiment can shield actors from this responsibility. Second, it makes the political domain a gladiatorial theater for contests of value or what Weber calls "warring gods." Third, it renders that theater a potential, though not inevitable, space for a post-nihilist recuperation and pursuit of value, even in the context of historical forces, both raging and quiet, that are destructive of value.

This chain of identifications also has implications for scholarship, curriculums, and pedagogy. It animates Weber's argument that developing and teaching knowledge must not be infected or inflected with values. If values are *now* inherently political because inherently contingent and partisan, then the slightest normative impulse is poison in scholarly waters. Representing more than bias or interest, this impulse brings undecidability, yes, but also force and potentially charismatic power into a place wrecked by the presence of both. Crucially, though, these stern demands for objectivity in research and analysis, and for value neutrality in the classroom, are themselves the result of Weber's post-foundational framing of values. No universal norms or transcendental moral commitments for him, no tissues of justifications to establish valid norms! Rather, values are fundamentally political *because* they are ungrounded today, because they cannot be secured by or as truth. Put the other way around, value deracination and contestability underlie the contemporary nature of politics itself, even as Weber never quite puts it this way. Warring values constitute the essence of political struggle for which power and violence are the dominant means. Far from seeking to solve the consequent irrationality of that domain, as we have seen, Weber dreams only of tethering it to responsibility, limiting its violence and keeping it away from laboratories of knowledge.

Values are political, politics is a field of power and violence, and scientific knowledge materializes only where all of this—power, passion,

partisanship, violence—is in abeyance. Weber famously inscribes this opposition in language itself. In the political sphere, he says:

> the words you use are not the tools of academic analysis, but a way of
> winning others over to your political point of view. They are not
> plowshares to loosen the solid soil of contemplative thought, but
> swords . . . used against your opponents: weapons, in short. In a lec-
> ture room, it would be an outrage to make use of language in this
> way.[27]

The language of seduction versus the language of analysis, words as
weapons versus words as plowshares, war and peace—the differences are
polar, not matters of degree. "*Whenever* an academic introduces his own
value judgment," Weber thunders, "*a complete understanding of the facts
comes to an end.*"[28] Impartiality, neutrality, adherence to facts and method,
are absolute opposites to the investments, demeanor, and effect of "the
prophet and the demagogue." One traffics in cool reason, the other in hot
passion; one seeks truth, the other power; one seeks to stir curiosity and
reflection in its audience, the other to attract followers.[29] Weber's fierce-
ness here would seem to be an eruption of that will to power we knew
would surface somewhere in the tightly disciplined scholar. It appears in
Weber's own ferocity about the methods for obtaining knowledge.

Yet again, Weber does not eject values from the knowledge field. This
would leave their power intact, a power that must be devitalized to insu-
late knowledge from it completely. Instead, he shifts values from the subject to the analytic object of knowing, even as doing so strips them of

their visceral and lived qualities, their emergence from the ineffable subjective sphere and their passionate deployment in the political one. Transposing the register of values from the knower to the knowable, and from belief or conviction to objects of study, brings them into a scientific domain that can reveal their inner logics and external implications *and* underscore their lack of foundation. Their magical powers are neutralized if not neutered by toppling them as "gods" and instead analyzing them as norms with assumptions and entailments. Weber goes further: the "meaning" of values is reduced to their relation to other values. As Weber puts it, the obligation of the scholar or teacher is to show that "if you choose this particular standpoint, you will be serving this particular god and will *give offense to every other god*." This is how "we can compel a person, or at least help him, to render an account of the ultimate meaning of his own actions. . . . And if a teacher succeeds in this respect I would be tempted to say that he is acting in the service of 'ethical' forces, that is to say, of the duty to foster clarity and a sense of responsibility."[30]

The mere possibility of such value-neutrality or objectivity in depicting or analyzing anything is widely and rightly challenged today. But this is not our main concern with Weber's wrestle to deploy objectivity to protect knowledge *and* value in a nihilistic age. Rather, what is striking is how values are transformed—even violated—by casting them as normative positions with analyzable precepts and logical entailments, by bracketing their psychic, religious, or affective dimensions, and also by lifting them from the very cultural and historical contexts that give them specific weight and meaning. Weber knows better. He is the master theorist of values as historical, protean, and ineffable, and of our attachments to them resting in sources that may be personal or transpersonal, experiential or theological. He knows well that values themselves emanate from cultural and political traditions, but also from desires, ambitions, hopes, delusions, resentments, rancor, revenge—all that Nietzsche depicts as the price of erecting ideals on earth. This attempt to make science useful to ethical, moral, and political clarity, and hence responsibility, thus transforms as it formalizes the object it studies. More, it aims to rationalize value itself . . . disenchantment's final frontier.

Weber is aware that the demand that the scholar and especially the teacher approach the study of values as contingent standpoints with inevitable entailments, oppositions, and exclusions both distorts and devitalizes the practice that he identifies with our deepest humanity, the practice of imbuing life with meaning and *deciding* what matters. Accelerating disenchantment, this demand converts worldviews into dry and disembedded normative positions drained of their captivating and motivating forces and their capacity to alter the meaning of history and the present. Weber requires that the academy be this drying shed and that the professoriat be Taylorized laborers within it, laborers who both stay in their own specialized fields and deny their own judgments or cares. Together, these strictures compose a more profound assault on values than even Nietzsche's demand for their genealogical revaluation—the latter leaves intact their seductive powers and weaponry while Weber's mandate aims to disarm them of both. And in direct contrast with Nietzsche's re-embedding of post-nihilist value in Eros and power, Weber treats values as if they could be evaluated according to rational consideration of their abstract entailments, even as he knows this is not how values, and the domain of politics where they are struggled over, works.[31] Thus do Weber's knowledge protocols simultaneously abet the emptying of the world of value, constrain the reach of human knowing, and transmogrify objects he promises only to study. These protocols employ the objectifying force of science to diminish what they cast as the subjectifying force of value—not only disavow value in knowledge, but deny value the status of knowledge.

Treating values in this way requires Weber to eschew Nietzsche's critique of accounts from nowhere, his eulogy for "the dangerous old conceptual fiction" of a "pure will-less, timeless knowing subject," with its "eye turned in no particular direction," and its attempt at expunging "the active and interpreting forces."[32] More than merely rejecting Nietzsche's radical interpretivism and exposé of the will to power at work in all knowing, Weber *demands* the very asceticism that Nietzsche diagnoses as the illness culminating in nihilism. If care for the world or agony about its predicaments may shape what we study, those investments along with all ambition for personal gratification must be abandoned *as* we study. Scholarship requires leaving one's beliefs and cares for the world at the threshold of research and analysis; eliminating personal expression from the work; adopting rational orderliness and method divested of one's person or personality; and of course accepting that one's endeavors may come to naught and one's "discoveries" will be eclipsed in time. In Wolin's words, "the exacting, even obsessive demands that Weber imposed on the social scientist form a counterpart of the Calvinist's adherence to the letter of Scripture and rules of piety prescribed by Puritan divines."[33]

In short, Weber *affirms* the "castration of the intellect," the "no to life," but also the "protective instinct of a degenerating life" that Nietzsche identifies with the ascetic ideal, its "program of starving the body and the desires" as the will to power turns against the life instincts themselves.[34] Nietzsche writes:

> An ascetic life is a self-contradiction. Here rules a *ressentiment* without equal, that of an insatiable power-will that wants to become master not over something in life but over life itself, over its most profound, powerful and basic conditions; here an attempt is made to employ force to block up the wells of force.[35]

Weber affirms this masochistic turn of the will to power against the self in intellectual life, and salts the wound by underscoring the fleeting quality of scientific achievement. The scholar as spiritless vessel of a meaningless cause requiring both self-negation and draining meaning from the world one analyzes—this is the ascetic practice Nietzsche predicted would culminate in "willed nothingness," a nihilistic spirit in the scholar aiming at stilling spirit in everything it touches.[36] Weber's own disenchantment thesis is too mild to capture what Nietzsche understands this practice to accomplish. Mystery and miracle, meaning and majesty are not simply subtracted from *the world* when it is subjected to the objectivist, ethically neutral scholar's scalpel. Rather, intellectual grandeur itself—in literature, art, and theory of every kind—is assaulted and reduced by the demands Weber makes on the scholar, demands to repel nihilistic effects in the academy. Yet this *drive* to diminish and reduce life, including the life of the mind, according to Nietzsche, is itself the drive of nihilism born from asceticism.[37]

More than merely proscribing a regime of spiritual-intellectual starvation, Weber builds a torture chamber for the man with the vocation for knowledge. This creature is condemned to the frenzied accumulation of facts combined with destruction of value at the heart of Weber's own diagnosis of modernity's slide into darkness. As Wolin writes, "Like the Calvinist [of the *Protestant Ethic*], scientific man accumulates" even as "what he amasses has no more lasting value than other things of the world."[38] Thus does Weber repeat in a scholarly register both the morphology of capitalism once its spirit settles into what he calls "mechanical foundations" and the morphology of depression induced by nihilism: driven but aimless, agitated and obsessive without outlets, desire raging yet choked, repose unavailable. With eyes wide open about the modern machineries killing human freedom, value, and satisfaction, Weber builds his cage of knowledge and scholarship from their blueprint: means separated from ends, the scholar reduced to a means, the ends receding altogether, a wheel of value depreciation whose turns we never get off. The de-spiriting of knowledge and the knower and conversion of the intellectual into a worker at the conveyer belt of scientific progress aim at draining not only meaning but emotional gratification from the work. The vocation demands both a spirit of kenosis and reconciliation to being eclipsed in the face of the inevitable obsolescence of one's production of knowledge.[39] In his demands for depersonalization, objectivity, hewing to method, and elimination of ultimate truth from scientific pursuit, Weber thus denies the scholar even the sublimated pleasures of creativity or imposing form on matter, and denies the pedagogue the hand in transformation that many associate with teaching.

Weber is fully alert to—and likely embodied with his own paralyzing depression—the tragic dimension of these demands on the academician, the machinery he feeds, the gratifications and redemption he denies. In many ways, the lecture on science is one long, depressive sigh about what scholarship is and requires, even apart from its miserable contemporary conditions. In this respect, it differs sharply from his depiction of the politician's life. While both vocations require that one "endure the fate of the age like a man" or else retreat "to the welcoming and merciful embrace of the old churches," science offers none of the compensatory pleasures of enjoying "the naked exercise of the power [one] possesses," giving one's own life meaning by serving a cause, or "holding in one's hands a strand of some important historical process."[40] There is no brave and exhilarating Lutheran moment of resistance, no "here I stand, I can do no other." And there is nothing grand to which the scientific activity is wedded, as the politician brings sobriety and restraint to passionate pursuit of a great cause. There is no world-changing purpose, hence no compensatory pleasures, to which the scholar weds the ascetic commitments of scientific method. The cause is science, full stop, a cause that is both unending and without ultimate meaning. Consequently, in contrast with the ethic of the politician, who must titrate principle, ambition, and responsibility, "the *only* morality" of the scholar "is that of plain intellectual integrity," and facing the ultimate meaninglessness of science requires simply "manly fortitude."[41]

Weber's distinctions and knowledge protocols would also seem to proscribe social and political theory that discards objectivism and empiricism for imaginative or speculative practices of knowing and thinking. We rightly draw on such faculties to conceive political and social constellations and powers, Sheldon Wolin writes, to produce a "corrected fullness" in accounts of political life that is required because we cannot "see" all political things firsthand.[42] "The impossibility of direct observation compels the theorist to *epitomize a society* by abstracting certain phenomena and providing interconnections where none can be seen. Imagination is the theorist's means for understanding a world he can never 'know' in an intimate way."[43] Such imaginative luminescence, with its dependence on unempirical architectonics and proximity to creative world-making in thought, is precisely what Weber aims to purge from social science, even as he admires it in literature, art, religion, and tradition. Imaginatively theorizing the world, despite Weber's exceptional talent for this work—exhibited in his accounts of rationalization, charisma, disenchantment, and more—without submission to method, is epistemologically unsound, unteachable, dangerous. We are limited to empirical studies, ideal types and typologies, and cool analytic dissections of culture and values. In his own version of purging the poets from the Republic, Weber further tightens the screw of asceticism and meaning-destruction.

In contrast with his crafting of *Beruf* for politics, then, which is positioned against the prevailing forces of his time, Weber draws the scholar's vocation into tight accord with rationalization and disenchantment, with value-slaying and machineries of domination built from calculative rationality. Far from contesting these, scholarly endeavor amplifies them with its commitments to specialization, objectivity, method, and dispassion. Thus does Weber decisively sever the Enlightenment link of knowledge to emancipation and bid adieu as well to the Humboldtian ideal of universities as builders of culture. He also barred the academy from practices of diagnosing social ills or crises, work we identify with critical theory and critical knowledge production. Thus, scholars in a Weberian mode are permitted to describe but not criticize an "information age" producing unrivaled capacities for surveillance and manipulation of subjects; an epoch of capital subjecting everything to the vicissitudes of finance; and knowledge so compartmentalized by discipline and so withdrawn from the world that it has little relevance to the crises of planetary habitability, humanity, and democracy now upon us. Weber saw the dark ahead, but his path to containing nihilistic destructions of knowledge and truth took us directly into it.

KNOWLEDGE AND RELIGION

> Release from the rationalism and intellectualism of science is
> the fundamental premise of life in communion with the divine.
>   —MAX WEBER

To this point, we have considered Weber's formulation of knowledge and requirements for producing it in terms of the opposition he posits between value-animated struggle in the political sphere and value-free knowledge accumulation in the scholarly one. This opposition is central to his polemic against politicized research and teaching. However, toward the end of the lecture, he moves from the problematic of political power to the problematic of the sacred, thereby transposing knowledge's opposite from politics to faith. The secular pluralization of values, he argues, sets up "battles of the gods" that science, and professors, cannot and must not settle.[44]

In the Introduction, I suggested that, for Weber, one entailment of rationalization and the nihilism it generates is the coming apart of knowledge, politics, and religion in modernity. These three domains are split off from one another only after science dethrones religious epistemological authority. Only at this point can knowledge be identified with objective, provable accounts (no matter what we think of this conceit). Faith rejects this binding of knowledge to objectivity and empiricism, which is why Weber, without malice, terms modern religious belief an explicit "sacrifice" of the intellect. Politics becomes a domain for struggle among value systems rooted in convictions that lack ultimate foundations. Religion and politics are both concerned with values, of course, but religion also claims truth, which means it risks encroaching on the territory of knowledge in a specific way that politics does not. John Locke's entire brief for tolerance of religious pluralism rests on the separation of these three spheres: knowledge is empirical and corrupted by power; faith depends on inner truth, conscience; and politics uses coercive power, which cannot produce faith or truth, only submission.[45]

For Weber, however, the existential threat of a religious attitude in the academy rests not only in substituting faith for reason or proof, but in a scholar's willingness to satisfy the great appetite for meaning among students in a disenchanted age. Weber knows that the absence of objective meaning is nearly impossible to bear, and identifies several strategies for refusing it. One is direct retreat into "the welcoming arms of the old church," where religious truth is absolute. He finds no fault with this but simply declares its inappropriateness in both the knowledge and political domains. Another is to adopt the bleakest iteration of nihilism, where nothing matters and life is pointless. Weber decries this move for its failure to appreciate that, in a secular age, each of us must *decide* what matters and what our lives mean. Still another possibility is making a religion of "everyday life" or "authentic experience," a tendency Weber sees as prevalent among the youth of his time and which he identifies with the "weakness . . . [of being] unable to look the fate of the age full in the face."[46] But the most dangerous infectious agent in the classroom is Tolstoy's question re-written: "'*who if not science* will answer the question: what shall we do and how shall we organize our lives?'"[47] This question bears all the desperation of the age, and in it Weber detects the longing for a prophet that many of his colleagues lack the fortitude and ego-discipline to resist. Students who want more than instruction in method, analysis, and facts, he fumes, are "looking for a *leader* and not a *teacher*."[48] A deflationary reaction to this longing, including explaining how it came to be, is all that we can provide. To Tolstoy's re-written question, then, Weber answers:

... only a prophet or a savior. And if there is none ... you will certainly not force him to appear on earth by having thousands of professors appear in the guise of privileged or state employed petty prophets and try to claim its role for themselves in their lecture rooms. If you attempt it, the only thing you will achieve will be that knowledge of a certain crucial fact will never be brought home to the younger generation in its full significance. This fact is that the prophet for whom so many of them yearn simply does *not* exist.[49]

Few things are more existentially difficult than confronting the absent givenness of what to value or care for in this world. Hence the many strategies for avoiding this hard truth—religion, nihilism, or the search for authenticity or a secular prophet. The task of the professoriat, Weber says, is to expose these for what they are and confront students with the innate meaninglessness of the world. Instead of filling that vacuum, we must teach that "life ... is the incompatibility of ultimate *possible* attitudes and hence the inability to resolve the conflicts between them. Hence the necessity of *deciding* between them."[50] Counterintuitively, only by affirming meaninglessness can corrosive nihilistic effects—spiritualization or politicization of knowledge—be averted.

Along with addressing desperation for meaning, there may be another reason for Weber's shift, in the final part of his lecture, from political demagoguery to false prophecy as a frame for criticizing value promulgation in the classroom. Even if politics is ruled out at the lectern, might ethical and moral teachings remain relevant? Against Kant and not only Nietzsche, Weber argues that ethics also lacks authoritative ground and cannot be arrived at through reasoning. Indeed, Weber sometimes appears to regard proponents of ethical or moral systems as even more irresponsible—perhaps because they are less ostentatiously partisan—than teachers who espouse political positions at the academic podium. The only ethical purpose for which the teacher or scholar can be of use, Weber says, is helping a student achieve *clarity* about the "ultimate meaning of [their] own actions."[51] Still, since value undecidability requires that each *decide* what is right and wrong, this service is no minor one. This "duty to foster clarity and a sense of responsibility" comprises both a pedagogical ethic and an action in "the service of [larger] 'ethical' forces" insofar as it furnishes students with the knowledge and understanding necessary to develop their own ethical standpoint. The decision itself is *not* scientific, but scientific analyses of different possible positions can enrich it. Here again, Weber struggles for a position in which values not founded in intellectualism may be developed and supported by it nonetheless.

As we take the measure of all that Weber prohibits in scholarship and teaching—diagnosis, critique, and advocacy on the political side, and shaping character and developing codes of conduct on the ethical one—it is important to remember what animates these prohibitions. Instead of deploying the academy to address the crises of meaning unleashing so many troubling forces in his time, he aims to protect academia from those forces. Although his position is recognizable as a "conservative" one, above all it is the academy he aims to conserve by protecting it from encroachments and deformation by capitalism, state interests, politicization from below, and religious impulses in any guise. But we must not mistake his position for that of Wilhelm von Humboldt a century earlier or that of secular liberals today. The prize Weber seeks to secure is not the Humboldtian university as a fount of national moral culture, nor is it faculty privilege or rights in the form of unregulated academic freedom. Rather, he aims to protect the academy's singular promise and purpose, its unqualified commitment to knowledge uncorrupted by power or interest of any kind, which paradoxically requires limiting the promise of what knowledge is or can offer. For neither faculty nor students does it provide meaning, moral truth, critique, or prescriptions for social, political, or existential problems. Yet in charting the world we inhabit, it is more than a pile of dusty facts. Without this charting, there is no hope of understanding, hence directing or re-containing powers otherwise dominating or threatening our existence. Moreover, knowledge production, including its challenges and limits, are at the heart of human intellectual development. Essential for individual self-crafting, this development is also indispensable for any possibility of crafting our lives together.

AFTERWORD | BETWEEN WEBER AND US

Against conventional readings of Weber's lectures on politics and knowledge as stipulating universal protocols, I have emphasized Weber's nearly hyperbolic efforts to protect knowledge and politics against their own late-modern conditions and effects. I have also been suggesting that his approach to nihilism's boundary breakdowns, its trivialization of fact *and* value, evisceration of depth and integrity, and disorientation about moral and political truth was a *pharmakon* in two senses of the word—scapegoating to produce order and a cure drawn from the poison. Weber's performative counter to nihilism's ablative force was to distinguish, separate, narrow, and quarantine. Knowledge gets rationality and secularism; politics gets charisma and its religious spirit. Knowledge is drained of passion, judgment, or ardor for a different world; politics runs on their fuel. Knowledge pursues truth, politics traffics in power. Knowledge is specialized, disembodied, withdrawn from the world; politics deals with the whole, the mortal and visceral. Weber moved against growing technocratic and bureaucratic forces in political life with a call for disciplined passion and purpose. He moved against romanticism in and politicization of intellectual life with a demand for nearly soul-killing Protestant discipline. He sought to infuse politics with the longing, heroics, and worldliness that he was determined to drain from the academy. The political realm needed to be rescued from its domination by inhuman machineries; the intellectual one from being overwhelmed by what he called the human element.

Intended to restore order and place when nihilistic decadence was destroying both, Weber's oppositions let the beast in by another door. As he submitted what remained of value to the grinding gears of disenchantment in the knowledge realm, he traded prospects for its transformation of the world for the magical force of charismatic leadership in the political one. He affirmed empirical study of the past and present while rejecting knowledge for developing critique or utopia. He pinned knowledge to the powers of the present, leaving only charisma in the political realm to break open a new or different future. In this, too, he kept education largely irrelevant to political transformation, preventing its synergies with mass movements and hindering its capacities to develop the desires and demands of such movements. Conservatism in one realm could not abet creative and transformational forces in the other. Indeed, to the extent that neo-Weberianism shaped the modus operandi of social science in the last century, it choked and scolded scholarly efforts at challenging or overturning the forces constitutive of our predicaments. To the extent that it captured an imaginary of the political centered on individual actors whose main stage is the state, it marginalized and even discredited insurgencies from below—social movements, protests, and experimental alternatives to centralized, undemocratic, or unjust institutions.[1] Instead, disruptions have been left largely to the acquisitive drives of markets and technology, and to leaders and movements generally devoid of the qualities

Weber assigned to charismatic leadership, those of restraint, selflessness, responsibility, and a cause larger than wealth, power, or the self.

The distinctions Weber drew and policed for knowledge also deprived social science of intellectual mediums through which to fathom modern political subjects constituted by complex desires, frustrations, wounds, reactions, fears, and anxieties. These may be subjects animated by abjection, rejection, subjection, or resentment as much or more than by interest, belief structure, or formation by particular types of authority. Weber's stipulation of academic purpose also gives up on developing an informed, politically engaged citizenry as an academic mission and agent of political change. It leaves that citizenry to its cultural-psychic stew of susceptibility and exploitability, and its fantasy that choice amid severe powers of domination amounts to freedom. In this, too, Weber barred academic contributions to post-nihilist world-making rooted in *popular* struggles over values reflectively established and also harnessed by accountability. Instead, his knowledge protocols meant that the academy would perversely withdraw from the world at the moment it was released from the Church. Specialized social science conscripted by methods grounded in Weber's value-neutrality and ideal types culminates today in mathematized models and experiments whose capacity for prediction in narrow domains and short temporalities cannot comprehend our existential crises of collective life—global and local crises of equality, democracy, and human and planetary thriving. These methods and models do not encourage questioning of the dominant discourses through which problems are identified and framed, or solutions outside of existing political, economic, and social terms and ordinances. As Marcuse wrote in the middle of the last century, this is social science that does not query but ratifies the status quo.[2]

Weber's opposition of fact and value, and treatment of the latter as a matter of personal conviction, also ignores how values acquire meanings and valences through the historically specific rationalities and discourses they intersect, and how, as they are actualized, other purposes and projects may transform them. Far from self-governing, the operation of values in political life is not simply supported by overt exercises of power, as Weber implies, but transpires within complex fields of power. This is why genealogies and discourse analyses are both vital to interpreting facts and values, and why what Stuart Hall, following Gramsci, termed "conjunctural analysis" is vital to understanding how values take shape in political culture. It is why norms in the political sphere do not operate as logical premises and entailments (as they do in philosophy), and why normative political theory of the pristine analytic variety is at odds with every credible ontology of the political. It is why "originalism" on both the Right and the Left is always only another political tactic, and why complaints about co-optation or weaponization of cherished ideals by opponents are both naïve and impotent.

In principle, for example, liberalism promises universal and equal protection of human dignity and liberty. In fact, this promise is contravened by liberalism's deep imbrication with powers organizing class, caste, colonialization, race, and gender. More recently, it is contravened by the tacit affirmations of hierarchy and inequality in its neoliberal iteration, and the xenophobic formations of its ethnonationalist version. Liberalism's account of liberty, which has no pure operation outside the philosopher's study, any more than socialist equality does, has not been co-opted and "weaponized" by the Right to wave free speech banners over Klan rallies, by corporations to dominate electoral democracy with their economic might, or by organized Evangelicals to erode sexual and gender equality. Yes, there are calculated, strategic moves here, but they are not outside liberalism's bounds; rather, they nest comfortably within and draw succor from liberalism's longstanding disavowal of social powers, and from neoliberalism's rejection of democratic legislation in favor of society ordered by traditional morality and markets. At the same time, these developments turn liberal political culture in a specific direction, one increasingly compatible with political authoritarianism. Just as we cannot think well about free speech today in abstraction from powers of contemporary social media or mobilized social supremacies, we will not think well about liberalism more generally apart from the plutocratic, xenophobic, nationalist, authoritarian, but also financialized and neoliberal anti-democratic formations providing its shape and content. While Weber's appreciation of how rationalities become forces and how instruments of freedom metamorphose into regimes of domination contributes to this kind of work, thinking conjuncturally—across dissimilar elements and seemingly heterogenous formations—and thinking genealogically—to grasp historical modifications of ideals, values, or principles in practice—is made difficult by Weber's epistemological and ontological hygienics and methods.

This example reminds us that a post-nihilist approach to values, in both knowledge and politics, requires more than reckoning with their lack of foundations, the disconnect between aims and effects, or their affective charge, important as these are. Rather, post-nihilist political and intellectual practices require grasping the embeddedness of political and intellectual endeavor in specific forms of governing reason and technologies of power, and grasping their intersection with powers and practices beyond those we are focused upon. That is, they require addressing the contouring of these endeavors by contextual elements not manifestly part of their own vocabulary or aim. What Weber sought to capture with his appreciation of political life as a field of action, contingency, and unintended effects, and with his development of an ethic of responsibility apt to that field, we need to bring to political and social theory as well. If politics is the wrong place for deployment of pure principle insofar as this deployment ignores principle's actualization by histories, powers, and effects of action beyond it, the same is true for scholarly political thinking and analysis.

Weber is certainly right about the obligation of faculty to teach students facts, including what he calls "inconvenient facts"—those that challenge received narratives or deep convictions. But we must also teach students about facticity, how facts come to be and acquire legitimacy as facts. We must introduce them to the complexities and contesting theories of how facts are constituted and interpreted, their inescapable historical, social, discursive, and hermeneutic dimensions, their non-isolability from one another and their lack of intrinsic meaning. In an age of so much confusion and duplicity about facts, science, and truth, what could be more important than exploring with students how these things are constituted, secured, destabilized, or superseded? Far from being dangerous, understanding the human creations and conventions here is a vital part of educating citizens and future scholars alike.

Weber is also right to insist that faculty are obliged to help students understand why no value system is ever true, but why, far from bringing analysis and judgment to an end or casting us adrift in relativism, this condition heightens the importance, indeed the urgency, of examining and deciding values—what to affirm, what to oppose, what to seek to bring about in the world. At the same time, it heightens the importance of understanding the complex sources of value constitution and attachment, value depletion, and the nihilism that follows, and of understanding why value concatenation is at once so intense and so shrill in our time.

Weber is right, too, to demand self-consciousness and care with regard to our own political views, and restraint in offering them in the classroom, even if this cannot be fulfilled in the way he demanded because, from Kant to evolution, climate change to genocide, gender equality to the Constitution, there are never facts or texts apart from interpretations of them. These, too, are cultural and historical, not only subjective, and practiced through languages of disclosure and occlusion, contextualization or emphases, and we have many measures of evidence, sound argument, and accountability by which to sift them, even if not to finally settle them. Weber is also right to worry about personality in the classroom substituting for teaching students how to research and think, even as personalities do not materialize or disappear on command, and of course are impossible to fully suppress. Socrates might provide a useful supplement here. Rather than banishing the personal charisma of the teacher, or what Socrates formulated as the transferential erotics cultivating desire for wisdom in the student, Socrates offered an ethic of restraint and responsibility, the very ethic Weber sought for political action. Once again, Weber's hard lines between the two spheres melt. And Weber is right to see the benefits of academic specialization, as well as its inevitability, yet we know the value today of liberating knowledge from some of the disciplinary silos and methodological lockdowns by which it is organized while retaining the value of scholarly discipline itself.

All this said, we have not spent this time with Weber only to correct him, which would be a strange and even silly academic exercise. As I suggested in the Introduction, he may help us right our own ship, or at least offer some help in navigating the storms. While acknowledging, for example, that knowledge and politics are in no way free of each other, he reminds us of the many reasons for protecting an interval between the political (and political-economic) and academic spheres, for not confusing or melding them. Intellectual analysis, discovery, critique, and reflection are fundamentally different from political action, legislation, and dicta: they mobilize different subjects and subjectivities; they draw on different languages, temporalities, aims, and ethoi; they have different requirements for realizing their potential. For this reason, demands that a curriculum comport with *any* political program—Right or Left, secular or religious—ought to be rebuffed with discussion about how such conflation corrupts both spheres. In addition to keeping political agendas and didacticism away from curriculums, scholarship today requires protection from being invested in or bought by the powerful, valued only for its commercial applications or job training, and from devaluation by anti-democrats aiming to keep the masses stupid and manipulable. One of Trump's most memorable moments on the 2016 campaign trail was his spontaneous cri de coeur, "I love the poorly educated!"[3]

While Weber exaggerated the opposition and the distance between universities and politics, he helps us see how the promise of each is threatened in an age of nihilistic boundary breakdown. Preserving the scholarly realm for the relative autonomy and integrity of thought, indeed for thinking itself, means resisting both hyper-politicization of knowledge and its structuration by relations of political economic dependence— state, economic, or philanthropic. Preserving the political realm for the struggle over values means resisting rationalization along with the temptations of both power politics and virtue politics. It requires renewing the value of values in the face of their nihilistic degradation. The struggle against nihilism is critical in both realms, but to conflate them is to lose the battle in advance.

Even with the world in an emergency state, then, where we may want every scholarly hand on deck, it is essential to have a moat between academic and political life. This moat is vital to protecting reflection, imagination, and accountability in knowledge production and dissemination.[4] It is essential to protecting an understanding and practice of facticity against indifference to it generated by nihilism but faithful to the complexity of knowledge formation. It distinguishes the place where values are struggled for from the place where they can be queried and analyzed, doubted, taken apart, reconsidered. Or, as Stuart Hall shaded the matter in discussing the difference between theory and politics, it distinguishes the theoretical domain, where we scrutinize the construction of facts, analyze narratives, and explore the inherent slide of meaning, from the political domain, where we seek to establish hegemonic narratives and arrest meaning's slide. Housing is a human right, trees have standing, no human is illegal, science is real, abolish the carceral state, this land is stolen, love makes a family—such claims cannot be subjected to fine-grained analysis in the midst of political battle but, along with challenges to them, must be opened and queried in academic analysis and in the classroom.

Certainly scholarly work, including that of theory and critique, can inform political struggles and help to develop their potentials or illuminate their weaknesses. The complexities of consent, autonomy, and choice; the slippery semiotics of corporations and personhood; the complexity of sovereignty claims; the ambiguous workings of human rights; the failures and aporias of constitutional democracy; the instability of racial and gendered identities: consideration of these may help build political projects and refine political positions. But that does not mean they can be aired in the midst of political campaigns, nor should they be confused with them. Just as nothing is more corrosive to serious intellectual work than being governed by a political program (whether that of states, corporations, or a revolutionary movement), nothing is more inapt to a political campaign than the unending reflexivity, critique, and self-correction required of scholarly inquiry. It is not a matter of being "too deep in the weeds"; it is a matter of the profound differences between the sphere where knowledge is achieved by opening up meaning and complexity, and the sphere where a political aim is realized through fixing meaning and reducing complexity. Scholars and students must allow productive disruption of their assumptions and axioms, and they must be willing to be uncertain and even bewildered at times. Political actors, on the other hand, must be steadfast, focused, and protective toward their purposes. Neither kind of activity should be scolded for its inapplicability to the other (as those who dismiss intellectualism often do) or submitted to the spirit and requirements of the other.

This is not a brief for arcane knowledge or ivory tower thinkers wholly unaccountable or indifferent to the world we live in. Rather, the point is simply that Weber's distinction between the pursuit of value codified as a cause and the submission of value to relentless intellectual scrutiny is ultimately far more important than his fact-value distinction in differentiating academic and political life. Indeed, the first distinction may help undo the second insofar as Weber's own hard codification of epistemology and method must, by his own account, be available to contestation, and hence to the surfacing of values in knowledge production.

Of course, relations between the academic and political realms are as important as the corridor of separation we have been discussing. This is especially true for democracy, which cannot survive an uneducated citizenry. Indeed, erosion of access to and quality of public higher education, as well as denigration of the value of college apart from job training, are underappreciated strategies of the combined neoliberal and right-wing assault on democracy of the past four decades. In a downward spiral, the anti-intellectualism that discredits education depletes capacities for democratic citizenship and makes citizens manipulable. In addition, academic specialization and professionalization, replacement of public with private research support, and neoliberal pressures on universities for immediate market deliverables have together diverted research and teaching from public, worldly purposes precisely when the crises of our time demand the opposite.

Given these recent histories, it may be that we have lately been too absorbed by issues of academic freedom while paying too little attention to matters of academic responsibility. The former is not trivial, especially given powerful right-wing campaigns to regulate curriculums and pedagogy. But might the latter address in a more profound and worldly way our imperiled collective future? Possibly the most important question before the professoriat today is not "what have we the right to say and do in or outside the classroom," but "what curriculums and pedagogies contribute to educating and empowering citizenries in these times?" How do we cultivate knowledgeable and thoughtful citizens in the short, fraught time and space of a college education, especially with so many other claims on students today? Ought we to reconsider the wide latitude offered to most university students in what they can study . . . and avoid studying? What pedagogical strategies, texts, topics, and discussions might help redirect the reactive personal politics in which today's students are steeped, to incite deliberation about the large-scale economic, political, social, and ecological forces and trajectories comprising the present and near future?

How do we break the siloization, professionalization, and instrumentalization of knowledge that makes too much academic knowledge unworldly? And how do we help students, faculty, and administrators alike shed the absorption with enhancing personal and institutional capital that keeps them loyal to this siloization, professionalization, and instrumentalization?

Essential to this work is turning hard toward rather than away from values in the classroom. By this I do not mean promulgating values. Rather, classrooms are where values may be studied as more than opinions, ideologies, party or religious loyalties, but also as more than distractions from the empirical, technical, instrumental, or practical. It is where they can be deepened as worldviews (or recognized as falling short of that possibility), analyzed historically and theoretically, and considered in the contexts of the specific powers that mobilize and transmogrify them. It is where they can be examined genealogically, culturally, economically, and psychically—for example, as complex reaction formations or theological remainders. It is also where they can be discovered in powers that disavow or consecrate them through feigned neutrality or objectivity, whether those of technocracy, algorithms, markets, or law courts. Above all, it is where they can be framed by responsible teachers as without foundations, yet all-important in both grasping and responding to the multiple crises of our time. Approaching values in these ways would constitute a vital counter to a nihilistic age in which values are trivialized and instrumentalized; a political age in which they are widely perceived as monopolized by religionists on the Right and secular righteousness on the Left; a capitalist age in which they are mobilized to expand market share; a technocratic age in which they are buried in platforms and apps; and a secular liberal age in which they are personalized and individualized. Re-centering the study of values in higher education would also counter the steady pressure on universities, especially public ones, to elevate voca-tional training and therefore STEM fields above all else, an elevation that gravely threatens the most important remaining venue for deep and in-formed reflection on the world, and one which could not come at a worse time in history.

If Weber worried about classroom polemics destroying conditions of objective learning and thoughtful deliberation, these are hardly the most serious threats to classroom integrity today. Nor, despite the hay made of it by the Right and mainstream media, are issues of triggering, censoring, or silencing truly widespread or important, especially outside the tiny universe of elite institutions. Rather, one quotidian depressant of intellec-tual seriousness among students is their absorption of the cultural-political depreciation of intellectual life combined with their anxiety about their individual futures, which often manifests as preoccupation with grading rubrics and techniques for meeting requirements with min-imal investment.[5] There are also the crushing effects of an unprecedentedly schismatic consciousness borne by contemporary university students. On the one hand, most have internalized the neoliberal mandate to calculate and titrate their every educational, social, civic, and personal investment, relentlessly tending their human capital value to build their individual prospects. On the other hand, most are alert to the looming global ecolog-ical, political, and economic catastrophes that make the world in which they are tending this value likely to soon crash out of the universe.[6] No generation has ever stared so directly into its own lack of collective future while managing such intense, complex requirements for building its personal and immediate one. More than "cruel optimism," this predicament is too much for many young spirits, essentially demanding that, with their heads down, they put one entrepreneurial foot in front of the other as if they were not walking toward catastrophe. Build your resume, cultivate your networks, find your mate . . . but also, save for an unaffordable home and unlikely retirement, plan for the end of democracy and an uninhabitable planet. Most young people are in a mode of pre-apocalyptic survivalism, as are we all to some extent.

One way we might address this predicament is to acknowledge it and break it open with deliberately post-nihilist questions for our students:

"What world do you want to live in?"

"How should or could humans order our common arrangements at this juncture in world history?"

"What table of values ought to organize our existence—Sustainability? Freedom? (What kind?) Mutual tolerance or recognition of differences? Equality? (What kind?) Families or alternative kinship? (What kind?) Meaningful work or the abolition of work? Religion protected or diminished? Worldwide institutions or local ones?"

"How have the powers and technologies invented and unleashed by humans produced specific ways of being human and of occupying and destroying the planet? How can we confront the fears and the despair related to our current conjuncture without being wrecked by them? What do we need to know and think about, hence to study, in order to address these and related questions in a deep and thoughtful way?"

Empirical analyses (how things are ordered and work now) along with historical and material analyses (what forces brought us to this pass and what powers organize it) are all critical in framing such questions. Psychology, sociology, and political economy are important in developing and complicating them. Literary, theoretical, philosophical, artistic, and other modes of rendering and interpreting the world are indispensable to addressing them, as is basic literacy in science, technology, and philosophy of science. Indeed, there is almost no part of the university curriculum that cannot be brought to bear on these questions, although the professional schools and pre-professional tracks may need the most help and encouragement in bending toward them.

Of course, students should not be expected to answer such questions but, rather, incited to ask them and assisted in exploring them. Our pedagogy should be aimed at illuminating what is entailed in developing and deepening them, what moors and animates intelligent ways of addressing them, and how they bear on the crises of meaning, effective agency, and futurity that most young people experience. In this way, we would be not only addressing student anxiety rather than shipping it off to the ever-growing college counseling industry but initiating students into basic practices of thoughtful citizenship. In addition to offering students the concrete knowledges required to understand their world, we would be teaching them what is entailed in arriving at deep and considered value positions that are essential to meaningfully crafting their own lives, to being intelligent participants in democracies, and to avoid imbibing the existing order of hegemonic values, or of shallow and hyper-polarized values, as all there is. Equally important, orienting some of our curriculum and teaching in this way could help dismantle the shrill and relatively anti-intellectual character of the politicized academy today, offering in its place more productive, and more intellectual, practices of relating academic and political life. Such work comports with Weber's argument for "fostering clarity and a sense of responsibility" in students, and it accomplishes two things his program does not: first, it aims to make students worldlier and to incite their engagement with the world, both as they find it and as they may imagine it otherwise; second, it treats values as ineradicable elements of learning about the world as it is, that is, as embedded in what he treated as the factual world. In both respects, it would be a steady disrupter of positivism.

It should be clear that this is not an argument to place the question, "What is to be done?" at the heart of college curriculums. Nor is it a brief for "tolerating all viewpoints" in the classroom, a conceit that diminishes rather than builds the stature of values insofar as it treats "viewpoints" as personal possessions like property rather than as worldviews with power entailments. Developing Weber's encomium to replace such tolerance with fearless scrutiny and hence a certain depersonalization of values would today include helping students see why highly personalized justice claims and values imagined as nearly written on the body are at once effects of neoliberalism and markers of a nihilistic loss of world and crisis of desire. These things require thoughtful and compassionate exposure if we are to pique student curiosity about understanding the sources and implications of their political claims and incite their interest in other modes of political thought, identity, and purpose.

Fearless, critical analysis of values, consideration of the knowledges necessary to form them intelligently, and identification of their importance to individual and collective freedom and futurity—these are hardly the principles by which most university curriculums are designed today. Apart from pressure from every quarter to turn all but elite institutions in vocational directions, putatively norm-free methods in mainstream social science, where values are treated as illegal aliens, actively discourage such concerns and approaches in social science classes and training. This is compounded in most approaches to studying social and political behavior, and also in mainstream philosophy, where values tend to be reduced to norms, norms to opinions, and opinions to surveyable attitudes.[7] Students themselves have come to expect teachers to deliver "information" (increasingly in bullet points) and have learned to be made nervous by large, unanswerable questions in classroom settings. And instructor "bias" tends to be narrowly cast as overt political statements, a narrowing that excludes modes of interpreting facts, the politics of methods, treatment of theory, and much more. In all of these respects, the mission re-orientation I am suggesting for liberal arts curriculums, pushing as it does against current forces shaping cultures of higher education, is revolutionary. And yet it was old, conservative Weber who inspired it.

What Weber calls "values" are insignias of human depth and capacity, emerging on the one hand from what he terms our "inner lives," yet entailing on the other visions that guide ways of being in common. In this combination, they mark something unique about our species, namely its potential for crafting a world in accord with what we know and believe. The possibility of enacting these visions is uniquely threatened by forces of modernity diminishing our capacity to craft our lives together—the giant machineries of domination Weber locates in capitalism and bureaucracy, supplemented today with digital technologies and finance. This diminishment is a striking form of unfreedom; our acceptance of it is an essential strand of nihilism. Culturing value, placing struggle over values at the heart of political life, alone carries the alternative to rule by these unchosen regimes of domination, by pure powermongers or by technocrats. In this respect, Weber's insistence on warring gods as the permanent essence of political life is more than a rebuttal to those who naïvely imagine a unified, harmonious afterlife of a revolution. It also stands as an anti-nihilist counter to Schmitt's infamous identification of political struggle with the friend-enemy distinction, Lenin's reduction of politics to "who-whom" (who will vanquish whom), and the classic realist position that politics is governed by objective laws rooted in hypostasized human nature. It was Weber's appreciation of the inherently creative nature of value, and politics as the domain for struggling over value, that also led him to reject the Kantian effort to ground values in moral universals, the Marxist effort to embed them in dialectical materialism, the Nietzschean effort to invest great individuals with their redemption after nihilism, and what would become the neoliberal surrender of values to spontaneous orderings of markets and moral traditionalism.

Yet, even as he rejected new foundations for values—whether rationalist, naturalist, theological, or neo-aristocratic—Weber searched for ways to make values accountable to thought and tether their enactment to responsible action. For all of his evident limitations in limning the kinds of social and political theory needed to apprehend our current conjuncture and the social and political practices required to renew possibility within it, he understood that rekindling the value of value amid its nihilistic diminution or destruction entails recommitting to our humanness in a double sense. Values carry our distinctly political capacity to craft the world according to chosen purposes when that capacity seems nearly extinguished by forces governing and often imperiling our lives and future. This recommitment also entails embrace of the purely human wellspring of values and embrace of our complexly human—intellectual, emotional, psychic, cultural, and historical—attachment to them. Far from the nihilism some impute to this embrace, it alone bears the promise of nihilism's overcoming.

INTRODUCTION

1. The University of Utah, Tanner Humanities Center, "Tanner Lectures Overview: The Lectures," n.d., https://tannerlectures.utah.edu/overview/lectures .php.

2. Many knowledge fields have contributed to these disruptions, among them critical science studies, ecological studies, feminist theory, and post-colonial and critical race studies. Derrida's critical work on the operation of binaries in logocentrism and Foucault's on discourse and rationality are also crucial forces in enabling these tectonic shifts in understanding.

3. Max Weber, "Politics as a Vocation," in *The Vocation Lectures,* ed. D. Owen and T. Strong, trans. R. Livingstone (Indianapolis: Hackett, 2004), 93.

4. William Callison, "The Politics of Rationality in Early Neoliberalism: Max Weber, Ludwig von Mises, and the Socialist Calculation Debate," *Journal of the History of Ideas* 83, no. 2 (2022): 269–291.

5. Robert Eden, *Political Leadership and Nihilism: A Study of Weber and Nietzsche* (Gainesville: University Presses of Florida, 1984), 1.

6. Max Weber, "'Objectivity' in Social Science and Social Policy," in *The Methodology of the Social Sciences,* ed. and trans. E. Shils and H. Finch (New York: Free Press, 1949; New York: Routledge, 2011), 60.

7. Eden, *Political Leadership.*

8. Eden, *Political Leadership,* 188.

9. In the United States today, Bernie Sanders, Alexandra Ocasio-Cortez, and Stacy Abrams are examples of recent "heroic" leaders on the left.

10. On Weber in relation to the German crises of liberalism, in addition to Eden, *Political Leadership,* see David Beetham, "Max Weber and the Liberal Political

Tradition," *Archives Européennes de Sociologie / European Journal of Sociology* 30, no. 2 (1989): 311–323.

11. Wendy Brown, *In the Ruins of Neoliberalism* (New York: Columbia University Press, 2019), esp. ch. 5.

12. Friedrich Wilhelm Nietzsche, *Writings from the Late Notebooks,* ed. R. Bittner, trans. K. Sturge (Cambridge: Cambridge University Press, 2003), 83.

13. On the relation of criminality and nihilism, see Maia Stepenberg, *Against Nihilism: Nietzsche Meets Dostoyevsky* (Montreal: Black Rose Books), ch. 1.

14. These verbs represent an array of possible responses to nihilism and are not interchangeable. Containing or repelling its effects is quite a different matter from what Nietzsche called "working through" nihilism. We will return to this in the Afterword.

15. Alexander Nehamas, "Nietzsche, Modernity, Aestheticism," in *The Cambridge Companion to Nietzsche,* ed. B. Magnus and K. Higgins, 223–251 (Cambridge: Cambridge University Press, 1996), 224–225.

16. Nehamas, "Nietzsche, Modernity, Aestheticism," 226, 230.

17. Max Weber, "Science as a Vocation," in *The Vocation Lectures,* ed. D. Owen and T. Strong, trans. R. Livingstone (Indianapolis: Hackett, 2004), 27.

18. Whether or not lobsters "feel," when a fetal heartbeat begins, whether sexual preference is inborn, socially formed, or chosen, whether or not markets distribute efficiently—all of these are irrelevant to decisions of value.

19. Friedrich Wilhelm Nietzsche, *On the Genealogy of Morals,* ed. and trans. W. Kaufmann (New York: Random House, 1967), 153, 155–156.

20. Weber, "Science as a Vocation," 17; and Weber, "'Objectivity' in Social Science and Social Policy," 53.

21. There are important differences between Weber's account and Nietzsche's: Did we kill God, as Nietzsche alleges, or did God decompose through the processes Weber names, rationalization and disenchantment? As for nihilism itself, do we will nothingness or fall into it?

22. In Weber's time, these machineries were bureaucratic states and capitalism. Today we would add digital technologies and finance.

23. One can see contemporary mobilization of religion in cultural and geopolitical struggles this way too: Judaism, Christianity, Hinduism, and Islam have each been mobilized in ways that debase their value status.

24. Wolfgang Schluchter writes, "In the disenchanted world, 'liberation' from scientific rationalism becomes the 'precondition of living in union with the divine.'" Schluchter, *Paradoxes of Modernity: Culture and Conduct in the Theory of Max Weber,* trans. N. Solomon (Stanford: Stanford University Press, 1996), 48.

25. This also suggests that the heavy play of religion in Euro-Atlantic politics today is an effect of nihilism, not its antidote.

26. Sheldon S. Wolin, "Max Weber: Legitimation, Method and the Politics of Theory," *Political Theory* 9, no. 3 (1981): 401–424, 408.

27. Wolin, "Max Weber," 409.

28. Mark Warren, "Max Weber's Liberalism for a Nietzschean World," *American Political Science Review* 82, no. 1 (1988): 31–50, 32.

29. The work of thinking with Weber does not mean that his conservative, masculinist, nationalist, anti-democratic, and methodological investments can be sifted easily from the provocations we may find useful. These investments are part of the warp and woof of Weber's thought, and part of the worth and challenge of thinking with him.

ONE | POLITICS

1. "It's in a very particular interpretation, the Christian-moral one, that nihilism is found." Friedrich Nietzsche, *Writings from the Late Notebooks,* ed. R. Bittner, trans. K. Sturge (Cambridge: Cambridge University Press, 2003), 83.

2. Nietzsche, *Late Notebooks,* 146–147.

3. Nietzsche, *Late Notebooks,* 117.

4. Friedrich Wilhelm Nietzsche, *The Will to Power,* ed. W. Kaufmann, trans. W. Kaufmann and R. J. Hollingdale (New York: Random House, 1967), I.20, pp. 16–17.

5. Nietzsche, *Late Notebooks,* 219.

6. Nietzsche, *Late Notebooks,* 219.
7. Friedrich Wilhelm Nietzsche, *On the Genealogy of Morals,* ed. W. Kaufmann, trans. W. Kaufmann and R. J. Hollingdale (New York: Random House, 1967), "Preface," 16–20.
8. Nietzsche, *Late Notebooks,* 146.
9. Nietzsche, *Will to Power,* I.62–68, pp. 42–44.
10. Thomas Hobbes, *Leviathan,* ed. C. B. MacPherson (London: Penguin, 1968), ch. 10, 151.
11. Nietzsche, *Late Notebooks,* 147–148.
12. Ron Suskind captures this turn in his account of the G. W. Bush presidency, including the infamous quotation, attributed to Karl Rove, about creating reality. Ron Suskind, "Faith, Certainty and the Presidency of George W. Bush," *New York Times Magazine,* October 17, 2004.
13. Again, the G. W. Bush foreign policy, with its admixture of faith and ideology at the core of its decision-making, anticipated what would become the more blatant disregard for facticity and truth rampant in politics today, especially but not only in the Republican Party.
14. Robert Pippin, *Nietzsche, Psychology and First Philosophy* (Chicago: University of Chicago Press, 2010), 51.
15. Pippin, *Nietzsche,* 19.
16. Pippin, *Nietzsche,* 29. Consider how this energy, which is anti-instrumental in every way, contests the rationalization and disenchantment of the world that Weber charts as a world-historical force.
17. Nietzsche, *Genealogy of Morals,* I.13, p. 45.
18. In addition to consecrating the individualism in overcoming nihilism that is also one of its effects, Nietzsche's several routes for working through nihilism all converge on affirming this life and this world, abandoning the life-negating search for value outside or beyond it. The notions of eternal return and *amor fati* both treat the health and strength of the human will as all that can convey us away from the life-negating trajectory, from religion to science, culminating in nihilism. Again, for Nietzsche, the scene for this overcoming is individual, cultural at best, does not look to politics for possibility, and is antipathetic to

democracy, egalitarianism, or social or political responsibility. All of these limit Nietzsche's modes of "working through" nihilism for purposes of democratic renewal or repair of the world.

19. Mark Warren, "Max Weber's Liberalism for a Nietzschean World," *American Political Science Review,* 82, no. 1 (1988): 31–50, 32.

20. Max Weber, "Science as a Vocation," in *The Vocation Lectures,* ed. D. Owen and T. Strong, trans. R. Livingstone (Indianapolis: Hackett, 2004), 23.

21. Robert Eden, *Political Leadership and Nihilism: A Study of Weber and Nietzsche* (Gainesville: University Presses of Florida, 1984), 137–138.

22. See, for example, Brian Judge, "The Birth of Identity Biopolitics: How Social Media Serves Antiliberal Populism," *New Media & Society* (2022), doi: 10.1177/14614448221099587.

23. Weber, "Science as a Vocation," 29.

24. It is important to distinguish this kind of politicization—of hairstyles or brands of beer—from the politicization associated with consciousness raising concerning class, race, gender, or unsustainable production and consumption practices. The former are trivial matters of taste made to stand in for politics. The latter are relations of power organizing life in common, the crucial subject of politics.

25. Warren, "Weber's Liberalism," 34.

26. Warren, "Weber's Liberalism," 35.

27. Max Weber, "Politics as a Vocation," in *The Vocation Lectures,* ed. D. Owen and T. Strong, trans. R. Livingstone (Indianapolis: Hackett, 2004), 67–72. Certainly Weber's rationalization thesis is meant to be ubiquitous, though he recognizes it will take hold in different ways and temporalities across different spheres. Fundamental features of politics, however, escape it: the elements of power, action, violence, and hence contingency constitutive of political life means it cannot fully give way to administration without extinguishing themselves. These elements amount to the qualified "autonomy" of the political even when actors are hamstrung by administrative and party machineries, even when it is plagued by the evacuations of meaning and saturation by bureaucratic mentality characteristic of modernity.

28. Weber, "Politics as a Vocation," 67.

29. Weber, "Politics as a Vocation," 77–78.

30. Weber, "Politics as a Vocation," 77.

31. Weber, "Politics as a Vocation," 78–79.

32. Weber, "Politics as a Vocation," 82–83.

33. Weber, "Politics as a Vocation," 93–94.

34. David Owen and Tracy B. Strong, "Introduction," in Weber, *The Vocation Lectures,* xlii–xlv.

35. For Weber, the human world is a made world, all the way down—from institutions and values to the politician with a calling. Some of this "making" emanates from the logics of historical forces such as rationalization or its embodiment in capitalism. However, some of it is initiated by action, which is why Weber insists that "what is possible could never have been achieved unless people had tried again and again to achieve the impossible in this world." Weber, "Politics as a Vocation," 93.

36. Max Weber, *Economy and Society,* ed. G. Roth and C. Wittich (Berkeley: University of California Press, 1978), 1112.

37. In *Economy and Society,* Weber writes: "[Charisma's] bearer seizes the task for which he is destined and demands that others obey and follow him by virtue of his mission. If those to whom he feels sent do not recognize him, his claim collapses; if they recognize it, he is their master as long as he proves himself" (1112).

38. Weber, "Politics as a Vocation," 76–77. For a discussion of political Kantianism, see Owen and Strong, "Introduction."

39. Such play dominates depictions of politics on contemporary television shows like *West Wing, Scandal,* and *House of Cards.*

40. Weber, "Politics as a Vocation," 92.

41. Weber, "Politics as a Vocation," 77.

42. Weber, "Politics as a Vocation," 77.

43. Weber, "Politics as a Vocation," 78.

44. Weber, "Politics as a Vocation," 77.

45. Much has been written about Weber's ethic of responsibility. See, for example, the introductory essays in both recent English translations of the

Vocation Lectures [see *The Vocation Lectures,* ed. D. Owen and T. Strong, trans. R. Livingstone (Indianapolis: Hackett, 2004), and *Charisma and Disenchantment: The Vocation Lectures,* ed. Paul Reitter and Chad Wellmon, trans. Damion Searls (New York: New York Review of Books Press, 2020)] as well as Shalini Satkunanandan, "Max Weber and the Ethos of Politics beyond Calculation," *American Political Science Review* 108, no. 1 (2014): 169–181; Corey Robin, "The Professor and the Politician," *New Yorker,* November 12, 2020; Antonio Vazquez-Arroyo, *Political Responsibility: Responding to Predicaments of Power* (New York: Columbia University Press, 2016). My exclusive concern is with the significance of this ethic as it emerges from and responds to a nihilistic age.

46. Weber, "Politics as a Vocation," 32–33.

47. Weber, "Politics as a Vocation," 90.

48. Shalini Satkunanandan offers a useful reminder that the ethic of responsibility is not a cost-benefit or efficiency calculation. The basic elements of politics, from action and power to its status as the struggle over "ultimate values," are incompatible with such calculations, which presume a rational and hence predictable order of things. Satkunanandan, "Max Weber and the Ethos of Politics," 170–173. Corey Robin understands Weber as responding not only to action as potentially producing the opposite of its intended effects but stymied by the weight of bureaucracy and institutions. "Where Machiavelli saw [the] gulf [between intention and result] as an opportunity for a more sophisticated agency, in which the prince produces an intended effect by deliberately doing the opposite, Weber possessed little confidence in the politician's ability to manipulate outcomes. The medium of political action—the bureaucracies of the modern state; the violent relations and imperial rivalries between states—was simply too dense." Robin, "The Professor and the Politician."

49. Weber, "Politics as a Vocation," 78. Nietzsche's influence is palpable. In *Genealogy of Morals,* Nietzsche writes: "The cause of the origin of a thing and its . . . actual employment and place in a system of purposes, lie worlds apart; whatever exists . . . is again and again reinterpreted to new ends, taken over,

transformed, and redirected by some power superior to it." *Genealogy of Morals,* II.12, p. 77. Machiavelli's attunement to the transmogrification of political acts into chains of unintended effects and even inversions of actor intentions may be seen as structuring the entirety of *The Prince.*

50. Weber, "Politics as a Vocation," 92.

51. Weber, "Politics as a Vocation," 92.

52. Following his denunciation of the "sterile excitement, aimless and unfocused romanticism" of revolutionaries, Weber writes: "Mere passion . . . cannot make a politician of anyone, unless service to a 'cause' also means that a sense of *responsibility* toward that cause is made the decisive guiding light of action. And for that (and this is the crucial psychological characteristic of the politician), a sense of proportion is required, the ability to allow realities to impinge on you while maintaining an inner calm and composure. What is needed, in short, is a distance from people and things. The 'absence of distance' . . . is one of the deadly sins of every politician. . . . For the heart of the problem is how to forge a unity between hot passion and a cool sense of proportion in one and the same person. . . . This can only be achieved by acquiring the habit of distance in every sense of the word." Weber, "Politics as a Vocation," 77.

53. Weber, "Politics as a Vocation," 94.

54. Weber, "Politics as a Vocation," 77.

55. Weber, "Politics as a Vocation," 92.

56. Weber, "Politics as a Vocation," 92.

57. Nietzsche, *Genealogy of Morals,* III.12, p. 119.

58. See Satkunanandan, "Max Weber and the Ethos of Politics," 174.

59. "An inanimate machine is mind objectified. Only this provides it with the power to force men into its service and to dominate their everyday working life as completely as is actually the case in the factory. Objectified intelligence is also that animated machine, the bureaucratic organization, with its specialization of trained skills, its division of jurisdiction, its rules and its hierarchical relations of authority. Together with the inanimate machine, it is busy fabricating the shell of bondage which men will perhaps be forced to inhabit some day, as powerless as the fellahs of ancient Egypt." Max Weber, "Bureau-

cracy and the Naiveté of the Literati," in Weber, *Economy and Society,* vol. 2, ed. G. Roth and C. Wittich (Berkeley: University of California Press, 1978), 1402.

60. Eden, *Political Leadership,* 186.

61. Weber, "Politics as a Vocation," 93–94.

62. Yet some who identify charismatic leadership with authoritarianism would tolerate technocracy in place of democracy, which today means being ruled not merely by economists, behaviorists, and bureaucrats, but algorithms.

63. This kindling of desire can happen in quotidian settings and institutions, and it is significant that the Right has organized for decades in schools, churches, civic associations, leisure pursuits, and, of course, media. The Left, notwithstanding Gramsci, Stuart Hall, and the program of the early Frankfurt School, has largely neglected the cultural production and dissemination of its values in this way.

64. This was the "polar night of icy darkness and harshness" that Weber forecasted for the near future, and which would soon materialize as fascism, national socialism, and war. Weber, "Politics as a Vocation," 93.

65. Weber explicitly affirmed the identification of the German university tradition with an "aristocratic spirit," not a democratic one. See Weber, "Science as a Vocation," 6.

TWO | KNOWLEDGE

1. Max Weber, "Science as a Vocation," in *The Vocation Lectures,* ed. D. Owen and T. Strong, trans. R. Livingstone (Indianapolis: Hackett, 2004), 20.

2. For this reason, in a recent English edition of Weber's lectures, translator Damion Searls renders "Science as a Vocation" as "The Scholar's Work." See Max Weber, *Charisma and Disenchantment: The Vocation Lectures,* ed. Paul Reitter and Chad Wellmon, trans. Damion Searls (New York: New York Review of Books Press, 2020).

3. Paul Reitter and Chad Wellmon, "Editor's Introduction," in Weber, *Charisma and Disenchantment,* x–xi.

4. Weber, "Science as a Vocation," 28, 30.

5. Weber, "Science as a Vocation," 20. Weber's lingering democratic principles shine through here: one should only speak politically, he implies, where others are equally entitled and able to speak back.

6. From the essay explaining the outlook and intentions of the journal of social science he co-founded, Weber writes: "The *Archive* will struggle relentlessly against the severe self-deception which asserts that through the synthesis of several party points of view, or by following a line between them, practical norms of *scientific validity* can be arrived at. It is necessary to do this because, since this piece of self-deception tries to mask its own standards of value in relativistic terms, it is more dangerous to the freedom of research than the former naïve faith of parties in the scientific 'demonstrability' of their dogmas. The capacity to distinguish between empirical knowledge and value-judgments, and the fulfillment of the scientific duty to see the factual truth as well as the practical duty to stand up for our own ideals constitute the program to which we wish to adhere with ever increasing firmness." Max Weber, "'Objectivity' in Social Science and Social Policy," in *The Methodology of the Social Sciences,* ed. and trans. E. Shils and H. Finch (New York: Free Press, 1949; New York: Routledge, 2011), 58.

7. Weber, "Science as a Vocation," 10, 13.

8. Weber, "Science as a Vocation," 20.

9. Weber, "Science as a Vocation," 25–33.

10. Weber, "Science as a Vocation," 37. "It can never be," Weber thunders, "the task of an empirical science to provide binding norms and ideals from which directives for immediate practical activity can be derived." Weber, "'Objectivity' in Social Science," 52.

11. Weber, *The Protestant Ethic and the Spirit of Capitalism: The Revised 1920 Edition,* trans. S. Kalberg (Oxford: Oxford University Press, 2010).

12. Weber, "Science as a Vocation," 11, 12, 19, 20.

13. Weber, "'Objectivity' in Social Science," 96. Even different value systems cannot copulate or miscegenate but must be appreciated as bound in an "irreconcilable death struggle, like that between God and the Devil" (Weber,

NOTES TO PAGES 70-71

"Science as a Vocation," 17). Values cannot be submitted to compromise, blending, or modification by one another, Weber implies, without being corrupted or destroyed.

14. Max Weber, "Religious Rejections of the World and Their Directions," in Max Weber, *From Max Weber: Essays in Sociology,* ed. and trans. H. H. Gerth and C. W. Mills (Oxford: Oxford University Press, 1946), 352. Weber writes, "[Religion] claims to unlock the meaning of the world not by means of the intellect but by virtue of a charisma of illumination."

15. That said, after the linguistic turn and the rise of behaviorism, maintaining Weber's corridors of separation requires jettisoning Weber's own frank acknowledgment of the ineradicable hermeneutic dimensions of facticity, of the infinite complexity of all human things, and even of the values necessarily driving every inquiry in the social sciences. The positivist social science ironically built in his name after these turns eschews Weber's own insistence on a great chasm between the natural and social sciences and especially the inappropriateness of imputing "laws" of behavior to the latter, and attempts to close it with a killing mathematization, and positivist methods so resolutely unhistorical, and so indifferent to the complexities of human language, culture, psyche, and power, that it will draw the scholarship designed to fathom human things ever farther away from prospects for redeeming the species, compounding the nihilism Weber struggled against with the mountains of meaningless data and analysis it generates. This is the nightmare, fully upon us now, that Weber sought to forestall with his category purification and border barriers, with a singular place for everything and everything in its place, with his arch oppositions between modes of understanding that he also sometimes acknowledged were separated by a "hairline."

16. Max Weber, "The Meaning of 'Ethical Neutrality' in Sociology and Economics," in *The Methodology of the Social Sciences,* ed. and trans. E. Shils and H. Finch (New York: Free Press, 1949; New York: Routledge, 2011), 3–4.

17. Weber, "Meaning of 'Ethical Neutrality,'" 4.

18. This is part of what underwrites Weber's own effort to craft charisma in political leadership as "responsible to its element," discussed in Chapter 1.

19. Weber, "Meaning of 'Ethical Neutrality,'" 9.

20. Weber, "Meaning of 'Ethical Neutrality,'" 3.

21. Weber, "Meaning of 'Ethical Neutrality,'" 5.

22. Again, Weber has given us a condition of crisis, born of historically inevitable conditions, which he proposes to address through stipulations and oppositions that he posits as factual (hence true), rather than moral or political (hence contestable), even as he acknowledges their historically specific standing and often places terms like "objectivity," "neutrality," and "living without illusions" in quotation marks, underscoring their permanently aspirational status.

23. He stipulates culture as a "finite segment of the meaningless infinity of the world process . . . on which *human beings* confer meaning and significance." Weber, "'Objectivity' in Social Science," 81.

24. Weber, "'Objectivity' in Social Science," 81.

25. Weber, "'Objectivity' in Social Science," 76.

26. This is why Weber refers to the twentieth century as a (shallow) return to ancient polytheism. Discussing the impossibility of deciding objectively what to value, of expecting value to line up with the good or the beautiful, or of ranking the value of different cultures, he writes, "conflict rages between different gods and it will go on for *all* time. It is as it was in antiquity before the world had been divested of the magic of its gods and demons, only in a different sense. Just as the Greek would bring a sacrifice at one time to Aphrodite and at another to Apollo, and *above all, to the gods of his own city,* people do likewise today. Only now, the gods have been deprived of the magical and mythical, but inwardly true qualities that gave them such vivid immediacy" (Weber, "Science as a Vocation," 23, italics added). Their lack of an inward truth is the sign that what was cultural has now become politicized.

27. Weber, "Science as a Vocation," 20.

28. Weber, "Science as a Vocation," 21.

29. More than merely irresponsible or exploitative of power differences (part of Weber's concern in "Science as a Vocation"), at stake is knowing itself.

30. Weber, "Science as a Vocation," 26–27.

31. Weber calls this a service to students, in which a student is helped to "render an account of the ultimate meaning of his own actions," and a service to ethics insofar as it fosters "clarity and a sense of responsibility." Weber, "Science as a Vocation," 26–27.

32. Friedrich Wilhelm Nietzsche, *On the Genealogy of Morals,* ed. and trans. W. Kaufmann (New York: Random House, 1967), 119.

33. Sheldon S. Wolin, "Max Weber: Legitimation, Method and the Politics of Theory," *Political Theory* 9, no. 3 (August 1981): 401–424, 413.

34. Nietzsche, *Genealogy of Morals,* 117–121.

35. Nietzsche, *Genealogy of Morals,* 117–118.

36. Nietzsche, *Genealogy of Morals,* 163.

37. It would not surprise Nietzsche that historicism, formal analysis, and even deconstruction have been wielded to neuter that grandeur in the humanities, even if this is not the avowed ambition of these approaches to humanistic knowing.

38. Wolin, "Max Weber," 413.

39. One is not even a vessel in the Platonic sense because there is no communion with the Forms, no sensuous connection with ultimate truths.

40. Max Weber, "Politics as a Vocation," in *The Vocation Lectures,* ed. D. Owen and T. Strong, trans. R. Livingstone (Indianapolis: Hackett, 2004), 40, 76.

41. Weber, "Science as a Vocation," 31. Or as another translator, Damion Searls, renders this sentence, "in the lecture hall, simple intellectual integrity is the *only* virtue that counts." Weber, *Charisma and Disenchantment,* 41.

42. Sheldon S. Wolin, *Politics and Vision: Continuity and Innovation in Western Political Thought,* New Princeton Classics edition (Princeton: Princeton University Press, 2016), 19.

43. Wolin, *Politics and Vision,* 19.

44. Weber, "Science as a Vocation," 23.

45. John Locke, *Letter Concerning Toleration,* in Locke, *Political Writings,* ed. David Wootton (London: Penguin, 1993).

46. Weber, "Science as a Vocation," 24.

47. Weber, "Science as a Vocation," 27. Italics added.

48. Weber, "Science as a Vocation," 24.
49. Weber, "Science as a Vocation," 28.
50. Weber, "Science as a Vocation," 27.
51. Weber, "Science as a Vocation," 26.

AFTERWORD

1. The relentlessly pejorative characterizations of populism emerging from mainstream politicians, pundits, and scholars are an index of neo-Weberian hegemony in this regard.
2. Herbert Marcuse, *One Dimensional Man* (Boston: Beacon Press, 1964).
3. Libby Nelson, "The Strangest Line from Donald Trump's Victory Speech: 'I Love the Poorly Educated,'" *Vox*, February 24, 2016, https://www.vox.com /2016/2/24/11107788/donald-trump-poorly-educated.
4. It is crucial to avoid what Weber identified as the error of conflating intellectual concepts with what he termed the "density and chaos of reality."
5. Combined with growing reliance on Google for "research" of every kind, and the spurning of intellectual for technical knowledge, it is unsurprising that student expectations for learning in classrooms are at historic lows and that the question "is college worth it?" is routinely answered exclusively with data about the "college premium," that is, expected increased lifetime earnings.
6. Sarah Kaplan and Emily Guskin, "Most American Teens Are Frightened by Climate Change, Poll Finds, and About 1 in 4 Are Taking Action," *Washington Post,* September 16, 2019.
7. Responsible scholarship in the social sciences today surely means inquiring into how we came to our current state of emergency and being able to envision intelligent, viable, realizable alternatives. Without this, we especially frustrate students who look to the social sciences with the reasonable expectation that its disciplines will help them understand dire contemporary problems. The most serious and passionate of these students are often driven to the humanities, where their concerns and questions may be affirmed, yet detached from empirical study and analyses of history, social systems, and power.

ACKNOWLEDGMENTS

I am grateful to the Yale University Tanner Lecture Committee and especially Gary Tomlinson for inviting me to deliver these lectures in 2019. At Yale, Paul North and Kathryn Lofton engaged me in an exceptionally rich and challenging public conversation following the lectures. For critically engaging a portion of the work when I returned to it three years later, I thank William Callison, Jill Frank, Robyn Marasco, Matthew Shafer, Alicia Steinmetz, and Yves Winter. An anonymous reader for the Press made several fine suggestions that improved the book. For their generous and meticulous work on the final copy, my deep thanks to Judith Butler and Brian Judge.